I read Micha Boyett's journey i[...]ll, by which I mean anybody wil[...]ul language and riveting struggle [...]d is a deep, sweet invitation into God's loving presence. A must read for nonbelievers and believers alike.

—Mary Karr, poet and best-selling author of *The Liar's Club* and *Lit*

I devoured this kind and generous book: Micha is singing the longings of all the tired mother pilgrims. Our stories are finally being told, and no one tells about our prayers like Micha Boyett. Every word is like motherhood: elegant, earthy, loving, and present.

—Sarah Bessey, author of *Jesus Feminist*

With this beautiful book, Micha Boyett opens a door to Benedictine spirituality through which regular, busy people can enter and taste, see, smell, hear, and feel what it means to live life as a prayer. It's funny, encouraging, challenging, and relatable, the kind of book that stays with you long after the final pages have been read. This debut sets Boyett apart as one of the most promising new writers of a generation, and I am so grateful she used her considerable talents to reintroduce us to that long-lost friend—prayer.

—Rachel Held Evans, author of *A Year of Biblical Womanhood*

With grit and honesty, Micha pulls back the curtain on the beauty and liturgy of everyday life as a mother, a wife, and a follower of Jesus. Her memoir is a welcoming, inspiring read.

—Sandra McCracken, recording artist, producer, and hymn writer

Confession: I cried as I read the last page, sad that my journey with Micha and her prayers and her babies was over. A lovely, honest book.

—Shauna Niequist, author of *Bread & Wine*

Micha Boyett has crafted a memoir that will resonate deeply with every mother who has experienced the tension of loving one's children but also struggling with how this new identity as a parent changes every other aspect of one's life. Boyett does not hold back her fears, doubts, and struggles in her quest for a deeper connection to God, and her honesty gives readers permission to consider their own areas of spiritual pain and brokenness. Boyett's words, so beautifully wrought, offer hope, comfort, and healing to those who are not content to remain lost in the fog of the early years of motherhood. In *Found*, Boyett gives us a fresh depiction of the truth that if we seek God, we surely will find—or be found—by him.

—Helen Lee, author of *The Missional Mom*

For years, Micha Boyett tried to win God's approval through her works: first as a would-be missionary, then as a poet, then as youth group leader, and finally, as a mother. For years, she worked at prayer, too, played at it and performed it. But only after forgetting how to pray did she find its true nature. Boyett's lovely book is itself a prayer.

—Karen Swallow Prior, author of *Booked: Literature in the Soul of Me*

Micha Boyett has written a stunningly beautiful spiritual memoir. *Found* will resonate with anyone who has lost sight of who she is after taking on new roles or beginning a new season of adulthood—and anyone who longs for signs of God's grace and presence. You'll lose yourself in the story and perhaps, like Boyett, also come to find a new way to approach the divine.

—Jennifer Grant, author of *Love You More, MOMumental,*
Disquiet Time, and *12: A Daybook*

Tender and intimate, searching and true, Micha Boyett's journey is extraordinary because it is ordinary. She struggles with jealousy and doubt, ministry and motherhood—and her candor about her hopes and her fears is an enormous gift. She asks questions that many of us would never dare say aloud. And in her quest for answers, she helps us rediscover the power of prayer and marvel again at the mystery of faith.

—Jeff Chu, author of *Does Jesus Really Love Me?: A Gay Christian's Pilgrimage in Search of God in America*

The birth of a child often changes everything in a mother's life. In Micha's case, it left her fumbling for sanity and longing for a deeper connection to God. Micha's quest for a meaningful relationship with God inspires and convicts. It's rare to find someone with such keen determination to search for an authentic expression of faith. As a Catholic mom of five, I found much to emulate in Micha's delight with the Benedictine practice of faith - especially ordering our days around prayer. *Found* is a poignant, beautiful treasure.

—Elizabeth Esther, author of *Girl at the End of the World: My Escape from Fundamentalism in Search of Faith with a Future*

If a good memoir requires a relationship of trust between author and reader, then Micha Boyett has earned my full trust and attention. She writes with elegance and honesty about the search for sacred space in the midst of life— on the playground, in the kitchen, on the street. Her book speaks powerfully to one of the most perennial questions of all—how do we find God in the day-to-day mess?

—Andrea Palpant Dilley, author of *Faith and Other Flat Tires: Searching for God on the Rough Road of Doubt*

This book is stunning. Beautifully written, Micha Boyett's *Found* is a penetrating story, rich in humanity and faith, the kind of book that stays with you long after you've read its last page. Like Henri Nouwen and Madeline L'Engle, Boyett's spiritual journey is divinely practical, a relatable and potentially anointed narrative that renews, inspires, and reminds us that we are not lost.

—Matthew Paul Turner, author of *Churched* and
Our Great Big American God

I defy any parent not to be moved by, and relate to, the raw struggle behind Micha Boyett's diamond-cut prose. We all wrestle with the loss of self after parenthood, the questioning of purpose and identity. Rarely do we get to connect with those inner conflicts through poetry such as this. When I finished *Found* I was compelled to write a gushing, personal confession to Boyett about how she tapped into my own atheist heart. No matter what you believe, you'll want to do the same.

—Lauren Sandler, author of *Righteous* and *One and Only*

Reading *Found* is like taking a deep breath of grace. You'll hear the echo of your own questions and doubts in the gentle ways Micha Boyett addresses her own, and by the end, you'll feel the quiet goodness of enough. For anyone who's ever gotten prayer all tangled up in performance—this one's for you.

—Addie Zierman, author of *When We Were on Fire: A Memoir of
Consuming Faith, Tangled Love and Starting Over*

If you're like me, you've grown weary of a culture that demands the sensationalistic, the glamorous, the extraordinary. Micha Boyett is in search for the beauty in the everyday, the prayer that hides itself in dinners and diapers and naps. She is as skilled of a tour guide for Benedictine spirituality as she is for her own story, and in these pages you will find that the sacred has been there all along.

—Adam S. McHugh, author of *Introverts in the Church*

In *Found,* Micha Boyett tells the story of her own redemptions, inviting readers into a life of earnest spiritual seeking. Written in reflective bursts of prose mirroring monastic hours and the holy calendar, Boyett has created an account of spiritual resolve, believing that the most important journeys of the heart are the modest ones. And, in doing so, she has drawn a budding generation of contemplatives and prayerful practitioners a fine sketch of how to live a deep, prayerful existence in the world without a cloister or formal religious order.

—Dave Harrity, director of ANTLER and author of *Making Manifest: On Faith, Creativity, and the Kingdom at Hand*

In *Found,* Micha Boyett takes us from motherhood to monasticism and back again with the sensibilities of a poet, the spiritual inquisitiveness of an oblate, and the weariness and delight of a young mother trying to hold on to wonder in the midst of an ordinary and blessed life.

— Amy Julia Becker, author of *A Good and Perfect Gift: Faith, Expectations, and a Little Girl Named Penny*

Found

A Story of Questions, Grace, and

Everyday Prayer

Micha Boyett

WORTHY®
PUBLISHING

This is a work of nonfiction. The stories and anecdotes in this volume are true accounts drawn from the author's life experiences and have been reconstructed as the author has remembered them, to the best of her ability. In some cases, for the sake of the narrative flow, she has combined more than one conversation or adjusted chronology. Some names and details have been changed to protect identities.

For foreign and subsidiary rights, contact rights@worthypublishing.com

Published in association with Rachelle Gardner, Books & Such Literary Management, www.booksandsuch.biz

ISBN: 978-1-61795-216-6 (trade paper)
Cover Design: Susan Browne Design
Cover Image: Getty Images
Interior Design: Christopher D. Hudson & Associates, Inc.

Printed in the United States of America
14 15 16 17 18 VPI 8 7 6 5 4 3 2 1

For Chris, always

Contents

There must be time to work, time to study, and time to pray. There must be time to pray in solitude and time to pray with others. There must be time to be alone and time to be in community. There is a daily, weekly, yearly pattern of life in the monastery. Life is inextricably bound up in the alternation of day and night, of the changing seasons, of the ebb and flow of the seasons, of the changing shape of the liturgical year.

—Esther de Waal

Acknowledgments

I am indebted to Macrina Wiederkehr for her beautiful book *Seven Sacred Pauses: Living Mindfully Through the Hours of the Day*, which greatly influenced my section headings. A few of the poems I quote in those headings came to my attention through her book. Also, her descriptions of the focus and themes of the hours of prayer influenced my own.

This book was five years in the making. I owe much to early conversations with Amy Snell, Anna Kocher, Lia Howard, and Alysia Yates. From the beginning of this work to the end, I was held up and loved by dear friends in Philadelphia, San Francisco, and Austin, and also by the Mama Monk community. The City Church Moms' Group prayed me through my drafts and watched my kids when deadlines were impossible. To all who prayed, babysat, checked in, and cheered me on, thank you.

I'm grateful to Janie Sellers, Kristen Haller, Debby Bellingham, Katie McMullen, and Liz Aleman (as well as several other of my dearests in Yoobs), who allowed me to share bits of their stories in the moments they intersected with my own.

Bob Fink, this book exists because you believed I could write and told me so. Thanks for the long conversations in your office: for teaching me to shape an image and for giving me permission to see the darkness in myself and search for the light.

Mary Karr, thanks for that day when you challenged me to write the feeling of the Holy Spirit in my chest. This book has been my attempt. Gerry and the Laments, has any girl ever loved her poetry workshop as much as I loved you? I hope you see yourselves in my sentences.

Thank you to Addie Zierman, Andrea Palpant Dilley, Katie McMullen, Farah Marklevits, and Courtney Queeney for the long hours you spent combing through this manuscript. You did so much to help me shape this book, from the biggest details to the smallest. I'm grateful to the Christ Church writers' group for working through my early drafts, and to the Okay Jesus Fan Club and to Laura Turner for the last-minute help in finding a title. Also, Alysia Yates, thank you for your genius idea of ordering this book by the divine hours.

I'm grateful to Jennifer Day, Sue Ann Jones, and all the folks at Worthy Publishing who brought this book to life. And thank you to Rachelle Gardner, my always-faithful agent, for reminding me to take deep breaths.

This is a story of the growing up of my faith, and I would be remiss if I didn't thank the pastors who have led me into my hope in a renewing, restorative, life-giving God. Nathan Gunn, for teaching me the power of Shalom and the depth of liturgy. John Yates, for modeling wisdom and faithfulness. Beverly Berry, for our hours of contemplative prayer. Casey Dunn and Joe Bruni, for revealing a gospel richer than I ever knew I already held. Cliff and Christine Warner for reminding me that this story of Jesus is "true, all the way through." Chuck DeGroat and Fred Harrell, your words have settled so deeply in my soul. This would be a different story without your teaching.

Sunny and Aimee, thank you for reading, supporting, and celebrating with me. (Big) Brooks, thanks for inspiring me to listen to God's deep calling. And thanks for letting me tell some of your story here. Jason, from the poetry you painted on my walls, to the letter you wrote me senior year of college, to your always-willingness to help me get this book in print, you have been my greatest cheerleader. Every writer should be lucky enough to have a fellow-author for a big brother. Thanks.

I am also deeply grateful to my mom, dad, and my mother-in-law, Barb, who cared for my kids while I prayed with monks or hunkered down to write. Thank you all for loving me and the boys so well.

Mom, Dad, MeeMaw, PawPaw, Deenie, and Granddaddy: I believe in Jesus because you gave him to me. Thank you for the hymns, the stories, and the faith.

August and Brooksie, you had no say in whether or not I told this story, but here it is. I'm an imperfect mom, but let these words stand as a testament to this one true thing: I love you I love you I love you.

Chris, this is as much your story as it is mine. Thanks for letting me tell it. You and I are the only ones who will ever know all you gave so I could write this book. I will never forget.

And to Jesus, champion of the weak-willed: I believe in you. I do.

Foreword

by Ann Voskamp

I once stood to pray in a Benedictine monastery.

I had stood with these forty-seven men who had taken a vow of poverty, chastity, obedience, stability, to live a life of prayer. And there I was, the Protestant standing up to murmur prayers, the Psalms, seeking to be still long enough to know He is God— and discover what is only masquerading.

I had looked around at these men who knew something I was only slowly finding: one way to keep your life from crashing is to have hard stops—definitive times where everything stops and you pray. Times when you take your hands completely off your life and bend your knees to the One who holds everything in His hands. It was jolting, awakening, to bow in prayer with men who know that Jesus wants our worship more than our work.

One of the monks had read certain and slow from the book of Exodus. And all of me had listened, looking for the way through this thing that we are doing right now that is life.

How do you get through life knowing you didn't miss out being who you were meant to be? How do you exodus emptiness and meaninglessness and homesickness for something other? How do our days of hauling in the groceries only to find mold growing in the fridge, of sorting through piles of damp and reeking laundry, looking for underwear to wash before someone has to go buy some, of scraping burnt soup off the bottom of the pan and handing the kids peanut butter sandwiches instead— how does the ordinary invite us out of confinement and into a wholehearted life?

The monk then prayed Psalm 136. All of our voices had risen with, "Give thanks to the LORD, for he is good. His love endures forever."

And when the still fell deep and we let the silence come after the Psalm, my own pulse ringing, "Glory, Glory, Glory . . ." that is when I first noticed it.

I stared down at the tiles under my feet, under the monks' feet. I had stared down at cork tiles.

I had only actually seen a cork floor identical to this in one other place in the world.

In my kitchen.

On a hot night one August, in what seems like too many blue moons ago and a lifetime of dirty dishes and piles of bills, my farmer husband and I had laid down tiles in the kitchen— cork tiles. Because I had read somewhere that cork tiles were the best flooring to absorb sound.

My life is loud. We have a bunch of gloriously wild kids. In the heat of the moment, kids hollering, somebody crying, a back door slamming, I can stamp my feet when I should be biting my tongue. So we laid down cork tiles, this hope of hushed floors— quieter days. Though we had never seen another cork floor in our lives.

But now I had. Now I had seen cork floors a grand total of twice: under a life of prayers of Benedictine monks in a monastery in the middle of Arkansas . . . and under a loud and messy life of our flailing family in a farmhouse kitchen in the middle of ordinary life.

These pages in your hand?

They live in the space of that startling juxtaposition.

Micha Boyett writes brave. She stands with one foot in what we think God wants—and one foot in the mess we've got. She writes daring questions into that space, that space between the life we're living and the life we long to live.

It's too easy to live lost. Going through the motions. Feeling like you're straddling impossible divides with the life you want slipping like water through your searching hands.

Micha Boyett's words catch water. Her story, real and gritty, enfolds time into a cup to hold what matters. I read Micha's words and my breathing slows. She gives perspective. And hope. And a refreshing lightness to not take what doesn't matter too seriously. She revives: When you order the tangle of your days around Him, He untangles you. She moves: The moments all matter. The daily awareness of the small adds up to the whole of your life, and her words are like a dawn, stirring you to wake and walk.

To walk into a life of steadying liturgy.

Liturgy, that derivative of the Greek word *leitourgia*, the literal definition meaning public service. Liturgy, the public service of your life over the sink, the stove, the side streets, making all our moments this movement of holiness that moves the world in radical ways.

Turning these pages profoundly turned something in me: the only thing that prevents me from praying more is me.

Is it only my own inflated sense of self-importance, the elevation of my work, of my agenda, that keeps me from prayer—from the abundant life I'm desperate for?

Is the only reason I fail to pray—is it because I've made an idol out of self?

I felt hungry reading these pages, the knowing gnawing that prayer matters more than food, because my soul matters more than my stomach. These pages grabbed me, spoke directly into my starving places: a soul can shrivel up and die without prayer.

Without clarity. Clarity being ultimately that clear sense of calling that resonates through the walls and halls of a life.

Micha's wisdom absorbs sound. It absorbs the loud distractions. It absorbs noise.

So you can stand here—and hear. So you can stand and find that the place under your feet, right where you are, is holy ground that changes the world.

So you can stand and listen quite unlike you ever have before—

And find yourself found.

Preface

My first year of motherhood I lost prayer. I lost early mornings of quiet, mornings in my pajamas with a Bible in my lap, mornings when I spoke my mind's chaos into God's ear and let the chaos come back ordered, holy sealed. I lost peace. I lost clarity and certitude. My faith was never perfect before my son was born, but somewhere in that first year, somewhere in my distraction and exhaustion, I lost the Spirit life I had known. I blamed myself.

After our son August came, I kept waiting for prayer to return, waiting for prayer to be simple again. I wrote down names and needs, lists of people who deserved my prayer, and taped them to the nursery wall beside the rocking chair. I willed myself to wake early despite my fitful sleep the night before. I wanted to fix myself into contemplation, prove myself strong and capable of loving Jesus well.

But it never seemed to right itself again. If I woke early before my son, I usually stumbled to my praying spot and five minutes later was forehead down on the onionskin pages of Scripture, asleep. My mind was too fuzzy to offer anything. Other times, I did it. I gritted my teeth, threw back the sheets despite my four hours of sleep, and sat down thirty minutes prior to my child's expected waking time. And then, without fail, I'd hear his cry. If I waited till he was up, imagining some peaceful devotion in the rocking chair while I breastfed, his very living distracted me. My beautiful child. All I wanted was to watch him and let my mind be still.

I stopped praying in silence, in long, broad strokes of worship or petition. Instead, my prayers were little snaggled things, wads of yarn tossed up in place of something woven.

When I mentioned my trouble to other mothers, they nodded their heads with compassion. *Yes. That's how it is. It's hard to pray.* Some friends would preface spiritual discussions with, "Well, you know how it is. Prayer's not the same anymore . . ."

And I thought: *Is this it? If we wait until our kids are grown to pray again, won't we forget how? And if we lose prayer, then really, doesn't that mean we've lost God?*

When my son was only a week old, I read the preface to Kathleen Norris's *The Cloister Walk*. August was staring with unfocused baby eyes at my mother downstairs, and I was soaking in one of those post-labor Epsom salt baths, hoping for a small devotional moment, a distraction from the physicality of my new life as mother. At that point, my nipples were still raw and learning what they were made for, my body was still bleeding, and I was just happy to pick up a book that wasn't about breastfeeding.

What I heard Norris say in those few pages that day was so simple and challenging I spent the rest of the morning stunned by its implications. Referring to this world's ruthless urgency and how our culture "chews us up and spits us out with appalling ease,"[1] Norris describes a monastic perspective that perceives time as a gift to be welcomed, not an enemy to be wrestled.

I lay there in that bath, almost twenty-nine years old and soaking a body that had suddenly swung from incubator to night zombie, and felt God speak Norris's words into the empty place where my child had been: "The Benedictines," she said, "more than any other people I know, insist that there is time in each day for prayer, for work, for study, and for play."[2]

I thought, *I ought to remember that.*

I thought, *I need to believe that.*

PART 1

Vigils: Midnight

Prayer in the darkness.
Keeping watch.
Stillness.

What in me is dark, illumine.

—John Milton

1

Late November, Friday before Advent

I zip my fleece and turn back from the doorway of our barely-lived-in bottom-floor apartment, my bag already slipping off my shoulder.

"And don't let him run down the sidewalk. Cars just come out of garages. They don't even look . . ."

"I know, babe. I know." Chris is holding our eighteen-month-old son, August. He grins. I've already given my husband a ten-minute speech on our kid's needs and the dangers of diaper rash. Now I'm just being ridiculous.

"Okay." I look in Chris's eyes and breathe deep.

"We're good, honey."

"Yep. Okay. Yes." I kiss August on the lips, still baby-soft despite their slow conversion into boyhood. I kiss my husband and turn around as fast as possible so I don't change my mind. I walk down the granite stairs outside our building and yell, "Love you guys!" just in case they didn't hear me say it the eight times before.

Our street slants straight up one of the steepest blocks in the city to Coit Tower, with steps instead of sidewalk and huddles of tourists freezing in their shorts and T-shirts and complaining ("Who knew San Francisco would be cold?") as they pass our window with chins raised toward the climb. Two months ago, we moved across the country to this foreign city, this new life of sidewalks and bright green parks full of neighbors: one hundred elderly folks from Chinatown moving through Tai Chi in their jeans at 7 a.m., the hippie homeless dude with his bag of celery and carrots, and earnest thirty-year-olds with coffee cups and purebred dogs.

This life, my life, is one I never imagined for myself. This bright-eyed Texas-bred Baptist had finally found a home in the hard-edged sophistication of the East Coast only to be jetted away to a new land teeming with consigned clothing and required composting and women in scarves. I might as well have moved to Europe.

I walk the three blocks to where our car is parked on the street—every parking spot a miracle—and throw my bag into the passenger seat. I'm quiet in the car for a moment. *How long has it been since I've driven alone? Months?*

Before I quit my career in youth ministry and followed my husband's job and our fearful wish for adventure out west, my car was always full: car seat, sippy cups, Cheerios. Also, sixteen-year-old girls and backpacks and Taylor Swift on the radio. My car was full; my life was full.

I drive alone seven hours south through land I hardly believe I live in. Not through West Texas, not through the Northeast where I'd spent the previous eight years of my life, but through the California middle on a path to the Benedictines, toward a secret hope of illumination this first weekend of Advent.

Saint Benedict, who established his monastic way of life fifteen hundred years ago, and the Catholic monks who follow his rule, have been speaking to me in piles of books on my nightstand for months. I come to them in search of something I don't know how to a name. I want an antidote for my prayerlessness. I long to experience God again.

The prophet Jeremiah said, "Stand at the crossroads and look; ask for the ancient paths."[1] I am an unknown speck on a highway through gold mountains, at the crossroads between my twenties and thirties, between the life I imagined for myself and the life I am actually living, between our three-bedroom house outside Philadelphia and our small apartment in San Francisco, between the palpable sacredness of ministry life and the ambiguity of stay-at-home motherhood. I am living in middle ground, between the faith of my childhood—the Spirit who snagged the front of my overalls by God-hook and towed me to the altar for salvation—and the doubt of my mind, which though it has repeatedly seen the miraculous in the lives of the young people I ministered to, still struggles to believe the Spirit world is living and breathing, much less that I am breathing in it.

I drive through these hills so coated in gold and unaltered by trees that they must have been crafted by Spirit hands, glued down, glittered. The sun sets, and I drive into its shade, pushing my sunglasses to the top of my head.

I am a sometimes-believer, in love with Jesus. I am a mystic who can't grip tight enough to the mystical. I long for order but can hardly make a list. I need something ancient, not ruled by the culture that rules me, to tell me what to do when my boy is throwing a tantrum on the plane—thirty minutes of uncontrolled screaming, leaving bite marks on my neck to remember it by. I need to know how to love God when all I have to offer is my daily chaos. Mostly, I long to know a quietness in my soul, true contentment, despite my spiritual unimpressiveness. I need to believe that my simple life really is a gift and really can be holy.

৵৵৽

We all make vows, I think as I walk from my room at Saint Gregory's Abbey toward the chapel where the black-clad monk is ringing the bell for worship. It's cold in the desert. I pull my coat tighter, fold my arms around my body.

I stand by myself in the back and listen to the monks

chanting their way through tonight's selection of Psalms. In the front of the chapel, one monk holds the melody on a harp.

I glance around the pews at the other guests. There's an older couple from Pasadena. He's a retired religion professor from a nearby university and she's a feisty, compassionate type. She already forgot about the silence at dinner then winked at me when she realized she was the only person making noise. There are others, almost all fifty and over, maybe eight of us total, all here for similar reasons: time for prayer, a practice of silence, a chance to learn from people who have made a profession of contemplation.

The chants aren't hard to join. Generally, the monks sing the words to the Psalms with only the use of three or four notes. The sound is soothing to my overworked ears. *Three notes are just enough*, I think to myself.

What does it mean to be so moved by the contemplative life that person chooses this gathering and chanting and worshiping as his or her *work*? I find a seat in the last row of pews and let the music soak into me. Really, this is all I need: just this harp and these balding, mustached monks singing *Jesus Jesus Jesus*.

We all make vows. They made theirs to the monastic life: The order of eating and working and praying together. The common liturgy of Psalms on their lips and constant repetition. The hard work of living in community with people you didn't choose.

My brother painted the vows my husband and I made on two sheets of plywood that lean against the wall in our kitchen. "I will seek to encourage you with love and service and prayer all the days of my life," I spoke aloud in a meadow at the base of a mountain, flowers in my hair.

We make vows at the beginnings of things. We make vows

we intend to keep, and then we spend our days in life's middle, clenching them tight. How could we know what our vows mean until we've dug our fingernails deep into them all those years later? How can we notice the hard beauty of such words, the thick holiness of hope, until we experience what living a vow actually requires? Vows always demand an entire life. Even when they're broken.

I wanted a baby, but I didn't make vows to my son until, six weeks into my pregnancy, I entered into the unknowable illness that only the cell growth, hormone spike, and body shock of early pregnancy can provide. I retched and wept, lying on the couch some mornings until eleven, finally walking out the door to the office or the high school swim meet and vomiting on their respective parking lots. Everything in my body felt broken except for the warm spot below my belly where those dividing cells were shaping a human.

After weeks of feeling sorry for myself, it occurred to me that this was my motherhood boot camp, three months designed to snap me out of self-focused existence and into the reality of mama life. Each moment I bowed my head to the toilet, I was offering myself to this child. I was making my vow. Bearing and birthing a child is a much messier kind of vow-making than the sort I made in my white strapless wedding gown, but I made them both with the same solemnity, the same gentle naiveté.

Glory to the Father, the monks sing. I tap my head, the self-conscious touch of a Protestant testing out the waters of physical worship. *And to the son,* my hand drops down to my chest, that hallowed spot between my breasts—a secret valley where my baby rested his hand all those nights I gave him my milk at 3 a.m. *And to the Holy Spirit*, I touch the inner curve of my shoulder and carry it across to the other side. The covering of the cross feels holy here in this old stone candlelit room. The men in robes lead us out with their heads bowed, and we enter *the Great Silence*, twelve hours. We exit the chapel into the cold night and walk through tight black air toward our rooms.

2

Late November, Saturday before Advent

We spend the next morning and afternoon meeting in four different sessions with four different monks. Each shares thoughts on the season of Advent. This afternoon, we spend an hour with a young, handsome monk named Brother Michael. He says Advent is a season for vision, for seeing God at work around us. Prayer, he says, is how we encounter God. Prayer is how we see. He sends us out of the meeting room to spend twenty minutes alone practicing an Examination of Conscience.

I step outside into the cool California desert and walk toward the wooden chapel. The door is unlocked and the room is empty; wide windows high behind me pour in the golden shine of the coming afternoon sunset. I find a seat in one of the far back pews, every movement of my body echoing off the stone walls. I unfold my sheet of paper, the notes Brother Michael gave us to walk us through this prayer.

The Examination of Conscience, sometimes called the Prayer of Examen, is an ancient prayer practice penned by Saint Ignatius. It's a directed prayer aimed at allowing one's awareness to hover over the memories of the past day, a way to see how God has been at work, even when we didn't notice. This is a new way of praying for me, one that is less about the words I come up with and more about holy looking, the process of recognizing where God has been making himself known and where I missed God because I wasn't paying attention.

I look around. The harp is still where it sat earlier this afternoon during Sext, the midday prayer service at the monastery. The chapel is shaped like a cross: we regular folks sit in the bottom half, and the monks along the horizontal line. The harp is in the corner there, where the room breaks left, all those strings pulled taut between us as if to link the ordinary and the holy to one another. On the wall, above the place where the harp sits, is a candle, still lit. It is always lit, day and night. An eternal candle, replaced, I assume, secretly. Relit when no one is looking. Always burning itself through and always coming back.

Ignatius instructs us to look through the past day and simply notice: What was good? Where was God in the smallest moments? I kneel and lean my head forward, pressing my forehead into pew wood. I rewind my day, last night, yesterday, the night before. I think about Friday morning, when August woke too early, still on Central Time from our Thanksgiving trip to Texas. I went to him in his crib at 5 a.m. and lifted him out as he clutched his blanket and leaned back to find my eyes in the darkness.

"Hi," he said.

"Hi, baby. It's still night-night. It's still time for sleep," I whispered, pressing his head to my shoulder. I carried him from his room to mine.

He was ready to play but also hovering in that small window of sleepiness. I knew the only way to help him back to sleep was to bring him into our warm covers, to put my face in his hair, to smell him and woo him into sleep with snuggles.

I pause in that memory and look up at the crucifix dangling above the table, where the bread and the wine are carried forward and set before the hungry souls.

"Thank you," I whisper, my eyes open, my knees pressed hard into the kneeling bench behind the pew. "Thank you for how his hair smelled like baby shampoo and for how he slept in my arms. Thank you. I know he won't want to sleep next to me forever."

I think about sharing a bed with my husband on one side, his arm over my waist, and my child curled against my body. I think about the sweet, rumbled noises they make. I think about how much of my life is happening squished between those two.

The instructions Brother Michael gave us describe these moments of grace, as gifts from God, opportunities to become "more fully alive to God."[1] As I kneel alone in the dark chapel, I can't even work my mind through a whole day of searching for God's presence. I'm stuck at this one. This moment in the early morning with a curled-up toddler in his footie jammies and a long, lean man asleep on my other side.

I say it aloud: "You are growing me more fully alive." I pause and glance down at the yellow light puddling onto the floor beside me. "You are growing me more fully alive when I hold my child."

I sense a soft gathering of warmth between my lungs, a seed of grace thumbed into my soul's soil. *I don't yet understand, but I will.* I will understand that I've been encountering God despite myself, despite my failure at prayer, because of the good gifts I haven't quite seen it yet, this grace. I haven't noticed. But I will.

The eight of us come back together and sit in a circle with Brother Michael. He wants us to share what we discovered during our personal moments of prayer. A woman tells us about the grief she's experienced this past year, the loved ones she has lost. She talks about how she's coming back to faith even though she's been away for a long time. Then the professor of religion speaks. His words are intellectual. I track with him but tune out after a while.

It's silent for several seconds before I speak up. I say, "I'm here because I'm asking God to show me how to pray again." Heads nod. This crowd of Protestants and Catholics and in-between seekers is an interesting mix. Everyone is listening.

"My son is eighteen-months-old," I say. "And I feel like the past year and a half I've been a spiritual failure. I haven't gotten up early enough in the morning to pray. I've been obsessed with thoughts of my son instead of thoughts of God. I've started down a path that feels a little hopeless, like I can't figure out how to be a person of prayer and a mother at the same time."

They're all looking at me. All these strangers, age fifty and over, along with the twenty-something monk. They're all nodding their heads as if I'm making perfect sense. Although, of course, I'm not. How can I even begin to explain what lies beneath my prayerlessness? I was in ministry. Encountering God, teaching young people to encounter God, was my job. I've read the books. I know the verses. But despite my knowledge of prayer, despite my previous encounters with Jesus, I feel broken. Prayer feels broken.

I tell them about my time kneeling in the chapel. I say how I was stuck thinking of that moment in the dark early Friday morning. I say how I'm wondering if God may be at work in me in those moments of simple mothering even when I'm not aware of his presence.

"What if . . ." I say, then pause, looking around the room and locking eyes with Dina, the woman who talked and winked during dinner last night. I remember she's a mother. She might get what I'm trying to say. Dina nods her head, as if to draw out my words.

"What if those two people in my bed, those two gifts in my life, are not the people who *keep* me from prayer? What if they're the actual prayers I'm praying?"

I cry when I say this. I always have a hard time processing things out loud. My tears are inevitably connected to my voice, even among these strangers from Pasadena.

Brother Michael is thrilled by my thought. He immediately chimes in, "Yes! Yes, Micha!" Then he compares me to the Virgin Mother. Shocked at his own insight, his voice rises as he realizes, "Christ was *her prayer*!"

It's a lovely thought, that God's grace might extend even into my own prayerlessness, that God might take my meager offering of child-rearing and turn it into prayer, despite my lack of spiritual discipline. I want to believe him. I want to compare myself with Mary, Christ's mother. But instead I nod my head and smile while Brother Michael talks. And I try not to giggle. I chastise myself for my own cynicism. If only he knew how unholy mothering feels.

As a Baptist girl who grew up valuing Scripture above all else, I poured my natural love for words and story into the Bible at a young age. I spent my teenage years reading and rereading every biblical narrative in which a woman played a central role. I have pondered Mary's words and longed to understand her soul. And I have loved her.

I love Mary for being the original Christ-bearer. I love her Magnificat, the poetry of her prayer of praise and submission to God's work in her life. But I've never believed her life was perfection. I've never held her up as any holier than the rest of us. And knowing my mothering self, I'm quick to assume the kind of mistakes she probably made. I can only believe that if her son's life was her prayer, it was in spite of her failings. It was because of God's grace.

Actually, I don't even remember any accounts in the Gospels of Mary praying at all following Jesus' birth. Maybe Mary struggled to pray as much as I do. I think of all the stories of her life in Scripture, how she seems to be worrying in at least three of the biblical narratives that mention her.[2] Yes, she was a mother, probably an ordinary one, like me.

I imagine her smiling at Brother Michael's earnest attempt to give me hope. I imagine her face on the icon that hangs in August's room. She holds her son, her golden head-covering flowing into the Christ child's robe. She looks at me with those long, sad icon eyes then playfully winks, as if we're in this together, sharing a secret failed-prayer life. Mary and I are mother-friends, drinking coffee out of disposable cups at the park, sighing over how little sleep we got last night, telling one another how there is hope for us yet.

Even if Mary was able to make her mundane life as mother into some sort of mystic prayer, is that kind of prayer enough? Is raising a son and loving my husband really the only spiritual life God intends for me?

I want more. I want to be bold. I want to ask for miracles and see them happen. I want to join God in bringing healing into people's lives. The prospect of spending my next seventeen (or more) years as a passive child-raiser who prays mysteriously through the life of my child falls short. I like this idea that God is growing me more fully alive as I love my family, but I want to experience God at work in all of me, not just when I mother. I want a life filled with Spirit.

It's silent in the room and I'm suddenly aware that Brother Michael has stopped speaking and the odd collection of seekers has turned their heads toward me, awaiting my response. I smile at the young monk and his bright excitement. "Yes," I say. "That's a beautiful thought."

⊱⊰

Within these thin walls in the monastery's guest quarters, I sit on my bed, laptop resting on my legs. I hear my new friends, that couple in their seventies, talking about the session. They're discussing me. "I loved all he had to say except how he compared her to Mary. Now that's just silly," Dina says. I realize they're not adhering to the Great Silence, and I laugh to myself, wishing I could sneak off the monastery grounds with Dina and find us a couple of martinis. She's bold and friendly and unpretentious. Her husband, the religion professor, laughs too.

"Amen, Dina." I whisper to the wall. I'm frustrated that Brother Michael would call what I do at home all day *prayer*. What does he know of what it looks like to raise a kid? That night two months ago when August was getting a molar and he woke every two hours until I screamed at my husband at three in the morning and slammed my hand against a wall? *That, I assure you, Brother Michael, was not a moment of prayer.*

Maybe if I were more patient, if I were more gentle, if I yelled less or cried less. Maybe then God would bless my mothering and transform it into prayer. But right now, my parenting life feels far from sacred. I wipe my kid's butt. I cut his food. I sit on the floor and sing songs. I read stories. I'm *normal*. I'm not living some mystical mother prayer. I'm no Mary.

❧❧

I drive home from the monastery in silence, lonely for my husband and son but grateful. I've been reading about monastic life for a year now, longing for a healthier view of time, for contentment and inner order. This weekend has given me space to think. I spent only a day and a half at Saint Gregory's, but I saw enough of the monks' lifestyle to crave its simplicity for myself. The monks move back and forth from work to prayer, from prayer to rest. Five times a day they come to prayer, and always their pace is slow, deliberate. They work with their hands: one is a sculptor, others clean or cook, another does administrative work. I've always associated work with anxiety, with *hurry*. But I never saw one of them running from one place to another, stressed.

Maybe that's why I'm drawn to this strange throwback of an ancient practice. I long for that slow rhythm. They wake early. They stay close to home. They go out to work for small portions of the day but always come back to their central focus, prayer. Their tasks are daily and often mundane.

The connection hits me: A monk's life is more like a stay-at-home mom's than any other lifestyle I've seen. I live a rhythm too: I wake early. I feed my son. I play with him at the park. I change him. I feed him again. There's cleaning and reading and snack time and library time. We leave the house for the bank. We leave the house for the Moms' Group at church. Again and again, we come back home.

It looks so simple on paper. But for some reason my rhythm is frantic. Our schedule is full of toddler emotions and messes, phone calls and e-mails, toilet scrubbing, and my attempts at new friendships. The TV blares, the errands must be run, the phone screams with its relentless beeps. If the Benedictines really believe there is enough time in each day, I want to discover where all that time is hiding. Maybe it's hiding here in my schedule, in the midst of my anxious life.

Saint Benedict asked his monks to "hurry to the work of God."[3] The monks' central work is prayer. Though prayer schedules among the Benedictines vary from place to place, Saint Benedict listed eight times, or "hours," for prayer in his rule: Vigils, Lauds, Prime, Terce, Sext, None, Vespers, and Compline. When the bell chimes the hour for prayer, a monk heeds the call and returns to God's presence. Again and again, for fifteen hundred years, the monk has returned to prayer.

I can make my life like theirs, I realize. I think about my day at home with August, our liturgy of sorts: breakfast, play, snack, play, lunch, nap, dinner, sleep. What if every shift in our schedule was a call to prayer, a bell chiming my return to God?

Maybe, in the midst of all the distractions, I could hold an inner silence. I could ask God to show me where the time is hiding. I could look for it.

3

Late November, First Sunday of Advent

"Welcome home, Mommy!" my husband yells on behalf of himself and our son as I walk through the door around seven on Sunday night. August runs toward me and throws his body into mine. As I kneel down to him, I see a gash on his chin.

Chris reads my mind. "He hit the coffee table Saturday afternoon. He's fine. Right, buddy?" I pull August back again to stare hard into his broken skin. The tang of irritation toward my husband bubbles in my throat. Then a wave of guilt washes over my chest. *If I hadn't left,* I think as I finger that angry red line on my baby's face.

"Did you hurt your chin, Aug?" I ask. But before I can continue my blame analysis (*me or Chris?*), or mentally move on to why blame probably doesn't need to be cast at all, August grabs my hand and yells, "Come see! Come see!"

I step into the living room where Chris has pulled out the Christmas decorations and has already begun inserting the pieces of our fake Charlie Brown–sized tree into its metal "trunk." I love decorating for Christmas. I love warm twinkling lights and hot cider. I love cheesy Amy Grant albums and the goofy traditions my husband and I started before we ever had kids. Chris slides his arms through the weird appliqué women's Christmas vest he thrifted for a party a few years ago and has awkwardly worn every Christmas since. He hands me a child-sized snowman sweater and, when I start to take it from his hand, pulls me in into a hug instead. The skin on my face smashes against the plastic button snowman on his chest and he knows it, but he holds me there anyway. I give up the fight and lean in, relaxing against him. "I missed you," he says.

I lean my head back and he kisses me. I look up at him, my hands still around his back, my fingers intertwined. "Oh, I missed you guys like crazy. It was *so* quiet."

"Just what you wanted!"

"Exactly," I say and fall back into his hug. "That's why I loved it and hated it all at the same time," I mumble into his vest. Chris lets go and turns toward the stereo. "Rockin' Around the Christmas Tree" comes on, and I step back, the sweater still in my hand.

"Put on your Christmas sweater!" Chris yells and picks up

August. They dance around our tiny living room. Soon August is throwing decorative ball ornaments, and I'm laughing and dancing, trying to convince our little boy that these balls belong on the tree, which is, of course, totally illogical to him. We open boxes and pull out ornaments, a collection from the six Christmases Chris and I have spent together as a couple. I look at my husband. He says, "The monastery . . . really was good?"

"Yeah," I smile. "It really was."

4

Early December, First Week of Advent

I wake up early the first morning after my trip to Saint Gregory's, determined to get my body out of bed and into the quiet living room. My eyelids flutter apart and close again. I moan. And then my feet kick off the sheets and beg gravity to make them useful.

It's six o'clock, and I have my Bible and a few new books that I gathered from the monastery. I have a task now, a calling. I'm going to relearn prayer.

It's not that I believe Benedictine spirituality will be some magical answer to the spiritual sludge I've been trudging through. It's just that all the answers of my evangelical past— read more Scripture, pray longer, try harder, serve more people— have become heavy burdens in my life. I can't do *enough* to prove myself spiritually fit. And I'm not sure why I feel the need to prove myself at all.

I need a new teacher to hold my hand and take me to Jesus. Maybe Saint Benedict is that teacher. I guess it's not normal for an evangelical stay-at-home mom to consume every available book with "Benedictine" in the title. But I can't help it. I feel like I'm on a search for something, a spiritual antidote I don't know how to name.

I fumble through the bathroom and the coffee making and finally find myself on the couch in the living room in my pajamas, reading Psalm 10 in the warm light of the Christmas tree. I'm going to keep it simple. I'm going to start with the spiritual practice Saint Benedict laid out for his brothers sometime in the sixth century when he penned his "little rule for beginners" that would shape monasticism from then on.[1] I'm going to read and pray through the Psalms.

When Benedict instructed the monks in "the work of God," he assigned the weekly task of praying through all 150 Psalms in Scripture. When they gathered eight times a day in the oratory, the ancient monks prayed as modern monks continue to do: chanting the Psalms in unison. Modernity has brought with it a gentler approach to the Psalms. The monks meet for prayer only five to six times a day and cover only half the psalter in a week, but the Psalms remain their starting place, their way of prayer.

Maybe the Psalms are my starting place too. After all, the Psalms tell my story, our stories: joy, doubt, fear, sorrow, questioning, worship, hope.

I need the Psalms to gather me, to meet me in my anxiety and the weight of homesickness I've been lugging around. I miss our old house and how August had a carpeted playroom; I miss my other mom-friends who cared about more than their child's development. (If I have to hear one more neighbor talking about her two-year-old's Mandarin class I might heave.) And I miss real friendships, the kind where you know each other's deepest needs, where you check in and pray and love each other's kids.

I'm lonely and fearful. But prayer can fix me. Prayer can teach me how to live with joy. I decide I'll read five Psalms a day. I'll pause my life and read a Psalm: in the early morning, at midmorning, at lunch, in the afternoon, and before bed. I want to discover them during snack time and lunchtime, when I feel great joy at being home with my child—and when I feel bored and exhausted and frustrated and alone. I want quietness in my heart, like a monk thirty years into his cloistered life: still and gentle and willing.

Benedict asked his brothers to "make prayer the first step in anything worthwhile that [we] attempt."[2] If a day at home raising my son is not worthwhile, what else could be? I write this down on an index card and tape it to the window by the kitchen sink. I want to remember.

5

Early December, Second Week of Advent

I meet my friend Kristen at the park. Her daughter Amelia is two days younger than August, and we've been happily hanging out at the ancient wood-and-metal playground structure since we discovered each other. What I'm loving about city living, especially in a neighborhood like North Beach, is that while the neighborhood feels like it's lacking in children, I know I'll find them all at the playground. This is the truest community gathering place I've known. No one has a yard; no one has their own space. There is nowhere else to go.

I wave at the moms and nannies whose names I can't remember even though they've told me more than once. I say hello to the few I do remember, most from the toddler library story time August and I attend every Tuesday. There's something satisfying about this kind of community. It feels quaint, like a small town.

Kristen is an architect who has arranged her schedule so she can spend two full days a week with Amelia. She's way smarter than I am, and her house is sleek and well designed. I've already spilled an entire cup of coffee on her white rug, but for some reason she still wants to be friends with me. She's one of those people who can get away with having a toddler and a white rug at the same time. Who are these people, and how do they survive?

I'm totally jealous of her. How is she able to work and be at home, able to think and create and have grown-up conversations all while being a good mom?

August and Amelia don't acknowledge each other much. They're too young to really play together. They start out side by side, but soon August is obsessed with stepping up and down the three wooden stairs and Amelia is piling sand onto the base of the wide, silver slide. I've just told Kristen about my recent visit to the monastery. She's not particularly religious, but she's kind enough to act interested in my talk of Jesus and this experiment with Saint Benedict. At least I think she's interested, in a you're-my-new-friend-and-I'm-glad-you-have-something-to-keep-you-sane way.

I tell her how I think moms have a lot more in common with monks than any other sort of lifestyle or career. "Think about our daily lives as moms," I say. "We're forced to move at the pace of children, slow and vulnerable. Kids need to stop for naps. They need snacks. They cry for a long time over something insignificant. Kids are totally inefficient, right?" While we talk, August and Amelia begin trying to climb the gleaming silver toddler slide. They're laughing and falling onto their tummies and trying again.

"Sure," Kristen says and nods her head. "They refuse to fit themselves into our schedules. They make their own."

"Yes!" I say. "So we have to learn to plan our days around the naps and the diaper changes and the meals. Not the tasks we have to accomplish. If I try to accomplish too much, I always feel like a failure. I've just been thinking it's the same thing for monks. Not the naps and diapers. But the lack of productivity."

"Okay," she says. "Explain."

August is in the way of a girl at the top of the slide. "Buddy," I say as I move toward him, "this little girl wants to go down the slide. You need to get off so she can come down."

We shuffle our kids out of the way, and Kristen finds a bucket for them to fill with sand. There's only one shovel, which I'm sure will result in disaster. But so far, August is letting Amelia use it. He's found an old plastic cup.

I turn back to Kristen. "How is it the same for monks?" she's asking again.

"Um," I say, distracted by August, who is tossing sand into the air so it lands on his and Amelia's heads. "We don't throw sand, Aug."

Kristen's waits for my answer.

"Yes. Monks. So their lives are structured in the same way as moms, right? The slowness and small details of ordinary life. Their lifestyle is totally countercultural, if you think about it."

Kristen nods her head. I continue. "Our culture says every-thing revolves around getting work done, producing something valuable. And monks say life revolves around prayer and stillness. Contemplation."

I always get a little nervous when I start talking about prayer with someone who doesn't share my beliefs, who probably thinks I live in a religious fantasyland. I stand in the sunshine and shield my eyes, moving my feet back and forth in the sand. For all my complaining about the constant fog and chill of San Francisco's weather, today is beautiful, in the high fifties and sunny. It's December, and I've still managed to take my shoes off at the park.

"So, tell me this. Do monks just pray all day? Cause, really, can anybody just pray *all day*?" she asks.

"Kristen!" I open my mouth as if I'm deeply offended. "You're totally forgetting about the beer!"

"The beer! Oh. Yeah. Monks make beer." She laughs. "So they pray and brew beer?"

"At least that's what they do in Belgium." I grin. "At Saint Gregory's, where I was, there were a couple of artists and a store-keeper and a plumber, I think. Everybody works. They just pray more often than they—"

August screams. One of his hands squeezes Amelia's arm while his other jerks the shovel from her. Kristen and I jump into the relational mess of our children. We separate, talk about sharing, and then distract, in that order. August is off to the swings.

Eventually Amelia follows, and Kristen is beside me again. I'm convinced that prayer is hard in the same way being a mom and having a conversation is hard. I can never finish what I'm saying to God before the child interrupts. And once I'm back in the conversation, I can never remember where I left off.

I was going to say how monks stop to pray the way a parent stops to wipe a nose, break up a toddler battle, or sniff a suspicious backside. Monks stop to refocus their hearts. We mothers can't help but hear the cries of our children. We know their shrill-pitched screams from across the playground. We stop. We refocus.

I've been wondering what might happen if all that stopping brought me into God's presence every time. It doesn't now. Right now, it simply distracts. But what if it didn't? What if my child's need for me prompted me to pray? Not with words. I can't hold words and August's need simultaneously. But maybe, I think, maybe I could hold God's nearness in my chest, in the place where the guilt lives now. Maybe God's nearness could sink into my insides. Maybe it could fix me.

What if every movement of my day prompted a response to God from my spirit, incense rising from that tender spot between my ribs?

"What do you do when you pray?" Kristen asks.

Now we stand in front of the swing set in the sand. A cloud has moved over the sun, and my bare feet are cold. We push the front of their kiddie swings, all rubber and grime, the metal squeaking each time they lift and fall.

"I used to just pray whatever was in my head. And then I had too many questions, and I got sick of asking them. The questions stopped feeling healthy. So I started praying in ways where I didn't have to come up with so many words anymore." I catch Kristen's eye to see if she's tracking, if she's annoyed by what I'm saying. She nods.

"Lately I've been doing what the Benedictines do, using the Psalms to give me words. I've been repeating them, like reading the Psalm and then whispering the words as prayer. Sometimes it's interesting because the Psalms can get pretty gritty." I push August's swing to the sky and watch it swoop back toward earth.

"Really?" she asks. "I've never read them."

"Well, they're complicated. There's a lot of praise and thanks-giving and all the things you're supposed to expect from a book of songs written to God. But then there's also all this rage and passion and doubt mixed in with the praise." I stop for a second to form my words the way I want to. I push the swing.

"I've just been thinking how sometimes the rage and passion and worship are all in me too. I'm complicated the same way, you know? Capable of holding faith and anger, hope and doubt, all at the same time."

Kristen looks at me again and nods her head. "It's a way to let your prayer be as complex as you need it to be?"

"Yeah," I say, surprised by how much her words make sense. Surprised by how the Psalms are giving me permission to ask hard questions and still find my way back to the hope that God is true and good. "Yeah," I say again. "I guess I read the words in my head. I read them to God. And then I hope they start to sink down to my heart."

I'm thinking of the way a garbage disposal sucks all the pieces that are floating in the murky water down into the drain. Except maybe I don't want prayer to be that violent. Maybe more like a Magic 8 Ball, where the word appears, floating, and then it bounces along the wall, getting smaller and smaller until it disappears. Maybe God's words will disappear into the quiet dark of me.

August throws his head back into an almost-backbend. Amelia laughs and tries to do the same. She's more worried about falling out of the swing though.

In my earlier Christian life, I was taught never to admit doubt to a nonbeliever, as if that admission might cement their unbelief, confirm their speculations of God's nonexistence or unconcern. Time has righted that tendency in me. I've realized that just about everyone is like me, second-guessing, longing for courage to find awe in the world.

What I don't say while we're pushing our kids' swings into the blue winter sky is that I'm grateful for the Psalms because most of the time I just want someone to hold my hand while I approach God. Sometimes I'm silenced by the thick haze of fear or doubt or sadness in me, and I need a friend to speak up on my behalf. Maybe the Psalms are becoming that friend.

We stand in silence for a while, looking past the green metal fence surrounding the playground where a bent homeless man is shuffling behind a grocery cart packed full of his worldly possessions. "Keep me posted on the whole prayer thing, okay?" Kristen says.

I smile at her. "For sure," I say and give August another shove.

He yells, "Up! Moon!" and he flies all the way there.

6

Late December, Fourth Day of Christmas

"Did you know Benedict started out as a hermit in a cave?"

I whisper this question with my mouth full of toothpaste, foam creeping out of the corners. It's past midnight, and we've just come back from an evening with friends.

"What?" my husband responds. He's leaning toward the mirror inspecting a giant pore on his forehead. We're squeezed shoulder to shoulder in the guest bathroom of my mother-in-law's house. This is the first time we've been back to Philadelphia since we moved. It's been a restful week. We've played with August and reconnected with friends. I've spent afternoons reading the Benedictine-inspired books Chris got me for Christmas.

"Benedict," I say. "Did you know he started out living in a cave as a hermit?"

"Huh-uh," he says, distracted by his delicate forehead procedure.

"Well, I was just thinking about how there's something to that. Something to this man wanting to give himself to God and trying the most extreme thing possible first. You know, starving in a cave, waiting for God to send a hawk with crusty stale bread?"

I lift a palm full of water to my mouth then rinse and spit. "I just love that he tried to live alone in a cave and suffer for Jesus, but somewhere in that time, he discovered God had something better for him in community. You know, before that, monasteries didn't really exist at all."

I tap my toothbrush against the sink and keep talking. "Everybody was just living alone in the desert, beating themselves with sticks and stuff."

I stare at him in the mirror. "You listening?"

"Yeah, Benedict was beating himself with sticks."

"No!" I laugh. "Not Benedict. Well, he did beat himself a little bit. But I mean all those guys before him."[1]

Chris backs away from the mirror and reaches for his toothbrush.

"Benedict was following that same concept though: the Roman, privileged type, running off to the desert. Giving up all his possessions and his career and offering his life to God."

"Was Benedict before or after Augustine?" he asks.

"I don't know. After. No. Before. I don't know."

He smiles in the mirror. He's making fun of me. "Tell me more, darling," he says.

My husband likes to use the word *darling*, partly in jest and partly because he knows I like it. I think he's closer to Jane Austen's Mr. Darcy than any other man I know. *Darling* is fancy. And my husband and fancy belong together.

"I'll tell you more. But you have to listen."

"Okay." He turns and faces me, sitting on the toilet lid like an attentive student.

"Thank you," I say, giggling. "All I was trying to say is that nothing has changed for believers. Back then, people felt moved to follow Christ, and they would read Jesus' words to the rich young ruler and want to do something big.[2] So they'd give up all they had and head to the desert. Maybe they just didn't know what to do except the most extreme thing."

"So you're saying they beat themselves to prove their commitment?"

"Yeah. Maybe. Maybe they waited in caves for miraculous food and tried to beat the sinful thoughts out of themselves because they really loved Jesus and it felt like they were making themselves worthy." I pause and wait for Chris to nod his head.

"I'm just thinking that maybe God used Benedict to reveal a kinder way in a time when no one really believed there could be any other way, you know?" I continue. "Maybe Benedict showed people that God doesn't necessarily want us to hurt ourselves. That God wants us to belong to each other."

"So following Christ doesn't have to be so radical?"

"Well, maybe what we think of as radical is actually the easier way," I say.

"Deep."

"Totally deep. Can't help it." I smile.

I have a lot more to add, but Chris is satisfied with the history lesson. "We done here, monk lady?" he asks. He stands to face the mirror again.

"You wish." I squeeze moisturizer into my palm and rub it on my face. "I'll finish tomorrow."

❧❧

Our trip to Philadelphia has been hard and wonderful. I've spent the week seeing friends and having coffee dates and coming home to find August bonding with his grandmother, making cookies and playing trains. The longer we're here, the more San Francisco feels like a weird dream I'm waking from. Chris and I are finally home again, and all the loneliness is just a thing that happened once.

It's the morning of New Year's Eve, and I wake to hear August calling from the other room. As I move to get out of bed, I hear my mother-in-law, Barb, speaking to him, pulling him from his travel crib. Barb implored me last night to sleep in and let her take care of him this morning. "You should rest while you can, Micha." She was scrubbing dishes, and I was drying them while Chris put August to bed.

"Are you sure? I don't want to leave you with all the hard work."

"Like reading stories with my grandson and making him oatmeal?"

I smiled. "Well, I was thinking, like, changing his disgusting diaper and reading the same story twenty times in a row."

"That sounds perfect," Barb said. And I knew she meant it.

We're only here for two more days, and I can already see how she carries the pain of our looming departure. During August's first year of life, she took care of him at least once a week while I worked. She had no idea how fast he'd leave her daily life. One year with her grandson was not long enough.

I lie in my bed listening to them and think, *She needs this time alone with him.* I lean back against my pillow and sigh. *We left her and took her only grandchild away.* I try to breathe deep again, force the guilt out of my lungs. Then I reach over for one of the books Chris got me for Christmas. I'm halfway through one on the life of Saint Benedict.

I skim over some of the same things I lectured Chris about last night. How Benedict was a student of rhetoric who was frustrated with the pretension and vanity of his educated, Roman subculture. How, somewhere around the year AD 500, Benedict followed his impulse to abandon academics, his family, and his position of privilege, all in pursuit of a life given to God. He packed his bags and left for a pilgrimage of holy emptying.

As I read, I stop to consider his choice to leave Rome, his home. *Did he ever feel guilty for leaving his family?* I wonder. *Probably not. He was a kid.*[3] *And he wasn't a mother.*

Tradition says that as Benedict journeyed, he left a few miracles in his wake. I'm afraid our stories differ there as well.

He eventually made his home in a rocky, mountainous cliff near a place called Subiaco and lived there three years, waiting for food to come to him, mostly from a kind monk nearby who secretly dangled stale bread from high above the cliff. Eventually, Benedict was discovered and then sought after as a holy man of God. When offered more than one opportunity to lead a group of monastics, Benedict finally submitted. He left his cave and built monasteries, one after another. Eventually, his experience running these monasteries led him to write down what he had learned, for the sake of the communities and the monks who would come after him, seeking to live a cloistered life.[4]

I imagine that in his religious culture of asceticism, community was often seen as the way of the weak-willed, those who didn't have the courage of belief to live in loneliness, wait for miraculous food, or devote whole days to prayer. There's not a lot of historical detail surrounding why, but for some reason, Benedict left his life as a hermit for the cloistered walls of a monastery. He changed his mind.

What shifted for him? Was the cave simply a tool to punish himself, prove his worthiness to God? Was he trying to relate to Christ by giving away everything, even relationships? Did those three years alone transform him to see something new of God's heart? Did wisdom lead him to a kinder, gentler way?

I set my book facedown on my lap and look over at my sleeping husband beside me. We're in the double bed he slept in most of his childhood, and his six-foot-four frame doesn't quite fit. His feet hang off the edge when he stretches out. But right now, he's curled up on his side, his face pointing toward my side of the bed, his dark eyelashes brushing the skin around his eyes where wrinkles are just beginning to form. He's peaceful. I wonder if this week at home has filled him with the same sort of guilt I feel. I wonder how much hidden worry he carries.

I reach over and touch my hand to his cheek and that jaw I love. It's almost a ninety-degree angle. I let my pointer-finger move against the curve of it.

For these past several weeks since my time at the monastery, I've read and prayed about how best to pursue God in a new, monastic way. I've thought about prayer practices and spiritual disciplines. But as I read about Benedict, I relate to more than his teachings. I connect to his story. I understand his urge toward desperate obedience.

I've spent my life begging God to make me good at loving Jesus. I think about Saint Benedict's manic gestures of commitment, how long I've strived to submit to my Christian culture's ideas of obedience to God. I come to the story of teachers who rallied "true" followers of Christ to chain themselves to trees in order to know Christ's suffering. I read Benedict's response: "Chain yourself to Christ instead."[5]

Maybe, fifteen hundred years later, my culture of faith is just as obsessed with our own sacrifices, with proving ourselves worthy of Christ. Our sacrifices are just a different kind of severity. Ours are promises like the ones I made as a teenager: promises to live a difficult missionary existence overseas, or give all my money away, or stay single my whole life so I wouldn't be torn between a life of faith and a life of family.

I look over at Chris again, then toward the framed picture of the two of us laughing on our wedding day moments after our first kiss as a married couple. I ask God, *What are you doing in me? What are you asking of me?*

God is silent. Downstairs I hear Barb and August reading his new book about sharks. "The bull shark is very fierce," Barb says. I hear August's voice in response. He wants her to turn the page.

"God, I think you're carving a long tunnel in me, toward something better than guilt," I whisper out loud to the room. I believe in grace. On my best days I actually believe there was a cosmic magnetic gathering that happened in Christ on the cross. In Jesus all ascetic suffering, all the sacrifices I ought to be asked to give, were collected and woven into him. Jesus suffered so he could overpower suffering. Because Jesus was not consumed by sorrow or grief, God holds out to me its very opposite. That's grace. In my head, I believe God is kind and gentle, even to me. I've stood before rooms full of teenagers and preached that. But still my soul's psyche has its own rules: I should suffer. I should work harder. My life should add up to enough.

Somewhere in those dichotomies, God is digging a long tunnel from my mind's claim of God's tenderness to my heart's veneration of *trying really hard*. I have spent so much of my believing life trying to chain myself to a rock in order to prove my love to Jesus that I may have missed the chance to be chained to Jesus instead.

I turn my book back over and fold down the top corner of the page. Maybe I've missed the point all along. Maybe being chained to Jesus doesn't involve a chain at all.

PART 2

Lauds: Dawn

Prayer at the first light of daybreak.
Hopefulness.

Not knowing when the dawn will come
I open every door.

—Emily Dickinson

7

Mid-January, Second Week of Epiphany

Saturday morning: August plays with blocks on the floor, and Chris returns e-mails. I iron. It's been two days since the earthquake in Haiti collapsed the entire island, and that devastation has been pacing in my mind since. Every shove of the iron across cotton heats my longing to do something, anything more than this. *What am I doing here?* I think. *Is this really me? A housewife ironing in my pajamas? Someone who truly cared would be there gathering orphans, setting up first aid stations, handing out food.*

I say it aloud, casually, my hand moving the hot metal over creases. I say how I hate that I'm standing at an ironing board, watching a football game, while in Haiti thousands, hundreds of thousands, are trapped under debris and dying. I keep thinking of a couple we knew at our former church. The man was a doctor who would leave soon after a disaster and rescue dying people. I can't imagine a greater, more significant task.

So I press the iron hard into the white cloth. I think, *If I were a man I might be doing that with my life, not ironing the duvet cover because our cat left poop on it this morning.* So when Chris responds that if I were working in a place like Haiti I wouldn't have him or August, I make a joke about it. I say something about how they'd be just fine, they'd find someone else to iron their clothes. He knows I'm kidding. But he stares at me three seconds too long. He looks hard at my eyes from across the room until I recognize what I've said. Then he glances back at his e-mail. I flash my eyes down at the duvet cover, smooth a crease with my hand.

I sit with my words for a day until Sunday morning worship during the passing of the peace, when I turn to my husband and say, "I love you more than my idea of being remarkable."

He gives me the *I know* smile, the one with lips pressed together and his eyes squinting sweet but ironic.

"Hey," he whispers when I hug him, "you are a gift to us. What you do matters."

I say I know.

I know. But also I long to rescue the crushed of this world. I want to do something great, not just live the same life as every homemaker in America, out grocery shopping on a Monday morning in her yoga pants. Do I believe there's some secret path to *valuable* and I'm mindlessly skipping down the wrong one?

I think back to God's long tunnel between my theology and my striving soul. *Maybe I want to be there rescuing people because I want God to like me most.*

I pray with the congregation. We cry out for those babies trapped in debris in Haiti. I beg God to send a rescuer.

For the poor and the oppressed, for the unemployed and the destitute, for prisoners and captives, and for all who remember and care for them, let us pray to the Lord.

Lord, have mercy.

8

Mid-January, Third Week of Epiphany

I didn't grow up with the seasons of the Christian year in my life. We celebrated Christmas and Easter, and my childhood church kept the year in other ways: the annual ice cream fellowship in the summer, the church picnic in Palo Duro Canyon before the start of school, Western Day when we donned cowboy hats and boots with a barbecue lunch. Otherwise, we lived in perpetual Ordinary Time, spending every Sunday morning, Sunday night, and Wednesday night within the walls of that red brick building whose halls I knew like my own home.

Now, in the dark months of the northern hemisphere's year, I've come to look forward to Epiphany, the Season of Light, when we celebrate the life of Jesus: his baptism, his teachings, his transfiguration. I remember when Mr. English taught me the word *epiphany* in my twelfth-grade British literature class. We were studying Shakespeare. I remember the taste of that word on my lips. Such a word for such a sensation: the gathering of truth inside until it erupts into knowing. Then, as a seventeen-year-old, there was so much to know outside of the world I'd seen and experienced. Mr. English described epiphany as the moment when reality is suddenly revealed, when the light bulb goes on in your head. It is Light arriving in the season of darkness.

Epiphany begins with the great journey of the Magi, following the star to the Christ child. We find Christ here, in these early nights, our children playing inside while the cold wind whips the fresh air they long for against the windows.

And in this season, we seek the life of Christ, the one baptized in the river, fulfilling the prophecies in our hearing, the one who says both, "I am the light and you are the light."[1]

I sit in the yellow glow of the early morning, one lamp on, rainstorm outside, wrapped in a blanket my parents gave me in childhood—brown and thick with turquoise dancing bears. (It's dreadful. It's my favorite.) It's quiet, except for the noise of people walking past on the sidewalk, where a large rectangular manhole is loose against the concrete. Every step across it makes a *clang-clang-clang* that reverberates through my first-floor apartment. I hold a cup of coffee and my Bible. August is still sleeping.

Chris is in the shower. He woke with a sore throat today. Of course, it has to be today when he'll be going to his third job interview with a company I've never heard of.

"I put my résumé out there," he said to me over dinner last week, "just to get some practice."

I stared at him. Blinked a couple of times. Said, "Wow." And stuffed more spaghetti into my mouth.

I wasn't really sure what he wanted my reaction to be. He's been unhappy in his job since we got to San Francisco. He loved his work before we moved here, when he was running a sales team in Philadelphia. It seemed like his company was a perfect fit. They recognized his potential. Chris was supported and challenged. He felt like he had a future there.

Our move to San Francisco was a promotion. He was taking charge of sales for an entire product, a new product. But it's not so easy to sell something (or encourage your employees to sell something) you don't believe in. The company that moved us out here four months ago with big promises has so far not fulfilled them, culminating in last month's pay decrease.

Chris has been slow to give words to the disappointment he feels, but I've learned how to read his face. Every evening for the past two months, he has come home from work and sat on the edge of the bed removing his shoes and socks wearing the look of a tired man. He's too young to look so tired. That shoe and sock removal has become a sad ritual of longing, something I haven't been able to understand.

That night last week, between his spaghetti bites and the declaration of a job interview, he softened his eyes and offered me a tight-lipped smile from the other side of the table. I know when he's doing his best to calm my heart.

"It's this start-up looking for someone to train sales associates. There might be an office in Philadelphia soon. We could go back."

We're both lonely. But four months in is never a good time to consider returning. We know it. It's January, and here in San Francisco the leaves are still green and the air is fifty-eight degrees. It has rained almost every day this month. This climate is new and strange and I never know whether to wear a sweater or a skirt. I still feel like such a stranger to the land, the weather, the people.

I thought about our house outside Philadelphia, where we planted that baby maple last spring. I thought about the way the yard looked when it was first coated in snow. How I bundled baby August last January and how he sat in his snow clothes and watched me shovel the driveway. I had planned to raise my babies there.

I stuck my fork in the spaghetti and twirled it. "Well . . ." I broke the silence, looking up at him with a smirk. "Of course they'll like you and your awesome man face. You're so freaking good looking."

"If only start-ups hired people for their amazingly good looks." He grinned back.

"Of course they do. It's completely unfair to all the smart people. Because they always hire you if you have a jaw like Superman."

"Is that right? You think I have a jaw like Superman?"

"Exactly like Superman, honey." I took another bite. "They'll like you. Of course they'll like you."

తా⌒స

I reflect on today's interview, sip my coffee, and look out our rainy window. Already a few people are walking on the sidewalk, clanging the loose manhole.

I wish we knew what we were doing with our lives. Chris is good at his job, but that can't be enough. He has to learn how to find his value outside of his ever-changing happiness quotient at work. He knows that. He knows his life has to be bigger than work. His value can't come from whether or not his product du jour is selling well.

I guess I'm living a parallel struggle. I am not my job. I am more than the uninteresting stay-at-home mom I chastise myself for being. Chris is trying to understand his usefulness in God's kingdom, and so am I. We're both going about it in different ways. We're both sad. I know he's searching for purpose and value, but I don't have any answers for him. I'm searching for the same thing. I'm asking the same questions.

Psalm 50 is open beside me. It's a beautiful and terrifying passage of God's power and judgment. God points to the burnt offerings his people have given in his name, but then asks for something bigger, something more demanding than a religious act of piety. God wants a sacrifice of thanksgiving.

I turn back to prayer.

But instead of thanksgiving, my mind wants to lay out fear after fear. What if Chris hates his job forever? What if no one ever wants to hire him again? I imagine today's meeting between Chris and the hirer. I think about what might be the right salary and sigh of relief. I daydream about moving back to Philadelphia.

The next moment I'm worrying that August will swallow a coin. Will I try to reach in and grab it? What if it doesn't work if I tip him over and pound his back and the coin is obstructing his air pipe?

I sip my coffee. I'm supposed to be praying.

A sacrifice of thanksgiving, the Psalm says.[2]

The quietness of this morning is healthy. I thank God for it. For the blanket with dancing bears, the rain on the window, the two loud tourists walking by outside, the coffee in my lovely white cup, that God is trustworthy (even for Chris and his career), that my son has so far never swallowed a coin.

Thanksgiving seems to me the opposite of fear, the opposite of loneliness. Maybe thanksgiving is an elixir for this feeling I have of homelessness: no place to belong, no permanence. Maybe thankfulness is difficult because it *is* a sacrifice. Every moment I break my mind from the present fear or tedious daily task or even from the feeling of joy and turn my thoughts into a thankful recognition of what God has done, I break down some fear-constructed wall. Maybe thankfulness is the only way to live prayer.

9

Mid-February, Ash Wednesday

Chris is working in Atlanta until Thursday. And I'm not letting his absence stop me from Ash Wednesday, my favorite service of the year. I hike straight up Telegraph Hill, pushing the stroller filled with all twenty-nine pounds of my favorite toddler to the Coit Tower parking lot. I'm sweaty and wheezing by the time we climb into the car. It's 5:38, and August and I are trying to make it to church by 6:00. We drive two miles through city traffic and miraculously find street parking at 5:57. I pull out the stroller. Another four-block walk. I hold my keys between my fingers just in case I need to key-punch an attacker on the dark, semi-unsafe street.

I'm still new at City Church, awkward, smiling hellos at familiar faces whose names continue to elude me. But as I fold up the stroller at the door, walk the basement steps hand in hand with August down to the nursery, five minutes late and proud of my almost-timeliness, I'm relieved I don't see anyone I know. I want to be alone tonight. I want to watch carefully. I want to ache a little.

I find a seat open on the left side of the room near the back. The congregation is singing hymns, rich words reworked to new melodies. There's a trio on the stage: a violin, a cello, a flute. How often am I in a sacred spot alone, at night, the city's lightscape through the sanctuary's windows casting gold across the room? I should honor this moment. I should make God some good promises.

❧

The practice of Ash Wednesday opens the season of Lent, a tradition that is fairly new in my life. I discovered it in my twenties almost two years after I graduated from college and six months after I left behind my life as a good Southern Baptist girl.

In 2002, I packed my car and drove with my parents through cornfields northeast toward some vague idea of my future as a poet. I was escaping Texas for an education I never knew I'd wanted. I was off to New York to earn my master's in creative writing for two reasons: One, the creative writing program at Syracuse University had accepted me. This is a truth that still boggles my mind, not because I own some false humility, but because my GREs were outrageously bad and my knowledge of poetry was mediocre at best.

Second, I moved to Syracuse because my plans to work in international missions had been thwarted by two encounters with God that seem incredibly strange to my present-day self. To explain these encounters is to sound as crazy as they felt. The truth? I sat at my apartment's kitchen table scratching words on the mission's application form and felt God set a Spirit hand on mine. Two years in a row, God stopped my hand midway through the form. I never finished either of them.

The second year, I sobbed on the couch until God lifted my head from the pillow and slid an idea into my mind, one I'd written off months before. For two years my undergraduate creative writing professor had encouraged me to apply to poetry programs, Syracuse in particular, because it was one of two programs in the country that offered full tuition to anyone accepted. The night I realized that maybe God had other ideas besides my life plan, I blew my nose, walked across the room to the computer, and looked up Syracuse's application process. I had six weeks to gather a manuscript of poems and take the GREs. I applied nowhere else, and Syracuse only accepted six poets each year. In April, they called and invited me to come.

My decision to move northeast shocked me as much as it shocked most of the people in my life. Up until that choice I considered myself en route to be the next great single female missionary. Lottie Moon, the famous Southern Baptist missionary to China in the nineteenth century, was my hero. And I was passionate about East Africa. I had been making this life plan since eighth grade. The book-hoarding, word-loving part of my personality had been so well hidden through my late adolescence and young adulthood that my sudden turn toward graduate school astounded many of the people who thought they knew me best.

That summer before I left for Syracuse, one year out of college, I flew across the world to Kenya for a four-week graduate course on African cultures and religions. This chance to study in

Africa came only after I'd decided to quit my job and move to New York.

On the plane, I got to know Janie, who co-led our course. She was my mother's age, a small-boned woman with salt-and-pepper hair who had spent most of her adult life as a Baptist missionary in Indonesia. Janie talked about God's view of women in the most liberating and newfangled ways I'd ever heard. During the monthlong trip, we memorized Psalm 19 together, and she would recite the passage, gently removing the pronouns for God: "The heavens declare the glory of God; the skies proclaim the work of God's hands."[1] I knew my New International Version of the Psalms, and I knew just where a *his* was supposed to go. So every time she altered that pronoun, I was mesmerized. I wasn't sure what to with a God who existed outside of gender, but I was drawn to the possibility.

Janie's theologically sharp mind was somehow critical and generous at the same time. I sat beside her as often as I could on the seventeen-hour flight. She asked me about the dreams I had for my life, about the poetry I was writing. I told her stories about my inexplicable love for Africa as a child. How earnest I was when I dressed in "traditional," (more likely offensive) "African" garb in fifth grade for career day.

"Janie," I said at one point when we were still over the Atlantic, hovering near the continent I'd colored pictures of and imagined myself living in since childhood, "in middle school I worried about all the things that middle school girls are supposed to worry about. How my face was too skinny and my teeth were too big. How my mom would never buy me a Dooney and Bourke purse and I'd stay a nerd forever. How Hannah Keller and the cool girls would probably push my bag off the table in the cafeteria again." I looked down and tried to scratch the remnant of my spilled coffee off my jeans while I spoke.

"It's just that I worried about Africa at the same time. I worried about hungry children with swollen bellies and yellow eyes. I worried that they didn't know about Jesus. I worried that I was supposed to do something."

I leaned forward and set my elbows on my knees. *I was supposed to do something.* I took a deep breath. It felt so heavy, the longing I had carried all those years. When I told my story to Janie, when I looked into her eyes and explained how God stopped my hand on the application forms, I saw she believed me. She didn't just think I was lazy or afraid.

I *was* afraid. I was afraid of moving to Syracuse. I was afraid I was choosing poetry over one day running an orphanage in Kenya because of an experience with God I would never be able to prove. I was afraid that such a choice was not simply less than spiritually impressive. It was selfish, secular, near blasphemous.

As I sat on that airplane next to Janie, looking from her to my lap while my right hand twirled the cross I wore on my left ring finger, I realized I was shedding myself. I was shedding a grand idea of myself. I was being humbled, made smaller. Of course, this was a whole-body shedding. And I was like a snake: its eyes always peel off first.

By the time Janie and I stared out the window over the changing landscape of the African continent, we had moved our conversation on to women and Baptist doctrine, how the denomination (for the most part) did not allow women to serve in leadership positions. Janie wasn't one to bash the middle-class white males who ran the Southern Baptist Convention. Instead, she told me how she read every piece of Scripture with a Jesus lens.

"Jesus loved women, Micha," she said. "And he empowered them and threw off cultural expectations. He taught women in a world that didn't allow women to be students. He spoke to them in public! He told them they were valuable."

Her East Oklahoma accent grew stronger when she talked about women and Jesus. She leaned toward me. "Micha, who found Jesus' grave empty? Who witnessed the angel and gave the first testimony of Christ's resurrection?"

"Mary Magdalene? And another Mary maybe?" I said, stammering to remember my Sunday school lessons.

"Any men?" she asked, her eyes growing wide.

"No, no men," I said. "Not at first."

"And don't you think that's subversive of God? In a time when only the testimony of a man was considered valid . . . for the gift of witnessing the resurrection to be given to women? To the 'nobodies'?"

I had never considered that. And I liked that word *subversive* to describe God. I liked it when God seemed just like Jesus.

"Of *course* God is *for* women," she said. "Of course God has work for us to do . . ." She looked out the window and sighed. She'd been back from Indonesia for three years after serving there for twenty, and I imagine she was still in transition herself, learning how to live like an American, learning how to live in God's kingdom and also under the leadership of broken human institutions, particularly an institution that appeared mostly unwilling to be as subversive as the God it followed.

That's when she brought up my coming move.

"Micha," she said, "don't give up on us yet."

By *us*, she meant the Baptists. "You know we need young people like you. Young people committed to Scripture and thinking. Young people who will challenge the church's status quo."

I'd considered before that I might not be able to find a Baptist church in Syracuse. I figured I'd make do. I figured I'd find a Bible church or a nondenominational church. But never had I thought I'd actually *leave*. Being Baptist was so tattooed in my way of experiencing Scripture and worship and community that her words surprised me.

I can leave, I thought, looking out the window at the rugged, red-brown terrain of whatever African country lay beneath us. *She thinks I might leave because I can.*

That moment, as I moved my eyes from the window to Janie and back to the window again, I didn't decide to leave the Baptist Church. I decided to read and pray and ask all the questions there were to ask. I didn't know how to find my way into a grown-up faith, but I knew I was ready to seek it out.

Three months before, the night I learned I'd been accepted into Syracuse, I stayed up late praying for God to show me the next step. Was I supposed to study poetry? *Really?* I wanted a *yes* branded onto the part of me that would always second-guess. I had been reading the book of Isaiah and came to a passage in which God makes a promise to the Babylonian king, Cyrus, who would one day free the Israelites from captivity.

> I will go before you
>   and will level the mountains;
> I will break down gates of bronze
>   and cut through bars of iron.
> I will give you hidden treasures,
>   riches stored in secret places,

so that you may know that I am the Lord,
the God of Israel, who summons you by name.[2]

I wanted confirmation that this was the way I should go, that I wasn't alone, that I didn't have to fear unwriting the story God was telling with my life. I'd grown up in an evangelical culture that often took God's Old Testament words and accepted them as personal messages. This passage felt like mine. I felt the words blow through my insides, hot summer wind whipping around and setting me at ease. It was a promise. Yes, a promise made to Cyrus but also a promise God was making to me all over again.

God was walking ahead, clearing a path for my future. I didn't know yet how that future would include confusion, doubt, and an entirely new way of understanding my Christian faith. I just knew God had said, *Micha, where you're going, I'm going too.*

I'd spent my life on flat, golden prairie ground. When I arrived in Syracuse, the hills and bright autumn trees stirred something new in me. My eyes couldn't hold the extravagance of all that color. Before telling a story, an author shows the setting: the grass, the houses, the light slanting through the window onto her great-grandmother's old breakfast table in the kitchen. Every morning during those first few months in New York, I was surprised by my setting. I woke alone in my own apartment with the Texas flag stapled to the wall. I woke to a land in which no one I knew or loved had made a home. I woke to a new story, and I was the main character fumbling through.

My first few Sundays, I visited almost every nondenominational and evangelical church I could find in the Yellow Pages. There were only a few, and after each visit, I never went back.

Then, sometime in October, a couple of friends invited me to their small Episcopal church. It was a lovely old building with only fifty or so people in the pews each Sunday. From my first week there, I felt at ease with its beauty and clumsiness. The singing was off-key and the melodies unfamiliar. The preaching was mediocre. But the church welcomed and cared for me. The pastor blessed me by name. And the people prayed out loud from their seats in the pews in the middle of the service: for each other, for the world.

I had come to Syracuse frustrated with the worship experiences of my young adulthood, experiences that felt more like musical performances than sacred gatherings. I was tired of slickness and programming and a culture punctuated by churchy clichés. I wanted worship to be a little awkward, unrehearsed. I wanted to feel my prayers braided into the multitude of prayers across space and time each Sunday morning. What I discovered at that church was something entirely new to me. It was liturgy.

I learned to kneel and say words out loud with the congregation, repeating the Apostles' Creed each week until I finally got it right. I never knew where anything was in the Book of Common Prayer, but the words we prayed were jewels. They felt wiser than anything I'd ever come up with on my own. I had always loved language and art, but I'd never found them in church before. Each week as I knelt at the altar to receive Communion, the priest would declare Christ's body broken for me, and I would hold God's story in my hand. That wafer was both God's flesh and my sustenance, all at once. It was art, and I ate it.

That year I experienced Lent for the first time. I'd spent my life only vaguely aware of the season. Easter had always been something I stumbled into. It would show up in the form of Peeps in the candy aisle at Albertson's, and I would have one week to get a new dress in time for a big church spectacular. But that tiny Episcopal church had an Ash Wednesday service, and I was drawn to all things symbolic. So I showed up alone and sat in the quiet candlelight and watched the solemn faces accept the ashes. In that candlelit chapel, I ran my mind through what I could release those forty days of Lent. What did I depend on most in my small, book-filled student life? *Coffee.* I took the ashes and gave up coffee.

Every morning during those six cold weeks of February and March, while the snow piled outside, I brushed the frozen white from the car windows so I could make it on time to teach my eight o'clock freshman writing seminar. And each morning as I entered my day without coffee, I thought of Easter. I longed for Easter the way I realized I should have always longed for Easter. *Resurrection is true, and it is happening,* I would whisper to myself, as if the cosmic salvation from Christ were occurring all over again, right then, in some realm and time outside my own. I was going to be rescued from my spiritual failure and loneliness. I was going to drink coffee.

Here in San Francisco, I sit alone at church wondering, *What should I give up for Lent that will help me learn to pray again?* I've made this grand commitment of praying the Psalms with the Benedictines, of returning to God in the rhythms of my life at home with August. Our daily movements were going to draw me to prayer like the chime of a monastic bell.

Whether it's because of my clumsy inability to hear that bell or because of my fear of it, I am not being drawn. Snack time, lunchtime, nap time, I said I would pray. But somehow at the neighborhood playground, August's grimy hands pulling dried green beans out of his snack trap are so far from my vision of a sacred moment that I don't grasp it. I don't recognize I've missed God until we're back in the house at noon, shaking sand out of August's sneakers at the door.

Really, how am I supposed to pray while I listen to other moms talk obsessively about preschools and make a mental note to roll my eyes when I'm out of their vicinity? How am I supposed to pretend this life as a stay-at-home mom is holy when all it looks like is *everyday*? The hours drip past, and they don't feel divine at all. And the idea of prayer leads me not to grace but to worried guilt.

Why am I making rules for my prayer time anyway? I'd hoped that giving myself a schedule of prayer would offer a plan, something tangible to help me connect with God again. But what I feel is not God; it's failure. Once again, I'm not the sort of woman I wanted to be.

Ugh, Lord, I pray. *I suck at this.* My head is bowed, my body folded forward so my forehead rests on my arms. I try to sing with the congregation. I mouth the words of the hymn, but my mind refuses to cooperate. Who am I to think this monastic experiment is possible? Who am I to attempt the Psalms? I focus my mind back to the words of the hymn, lifted straight from Psalm 130. "Out of the depths I cry to you, O LORD," the Psalm says.[3]

"God, what do you want to say to me?" I whisper, the only coherent prayer I've put together since this service began. A pastor stands to talk about the purpose of the ashes. I focus my attention on him. I consider my tendency toward anxiety, especially in prayer, the one place where I'm supposed to be free from it.

I watch as the congregation begins moving toward the front of the room. *God*, I pray, *I think I've confused your Spirit with my empty striving.* I ask God to say what I most need to hear. I ask God to tell me that I'm lovable whether or not I went to Africa or studied poetry, whether or not I stayed in ministry or stayed home with my son, whether or not I ever learn to pray or fumble through prayer for the rest of my life.

Then I sit, watching: row after row, the five hundred attendees slide forward in two single-file lines toward the four ministers in collars with smudge cans filled with the remains of last year's incinerated Palm Sunday leaves. Their thumbs mix the oils of our foreheads, dipping over and over and mingling us all together with those remains.

I follow the line of people to the altar, where a pastor marks me with ashes and recites the liturgy: *remember that you are dust, and to dust you shall return.* God holds up death to my face like a mirror. I see it in my pastor's eyes. I feel it in the living, porous skin of my forehead. The cross is made dark on me. I follow strangers back to my seat and sit, elbows on thighs, my smudgy head pressed into my hand.

I'm going to die, Lord, I whisper, my eyes open when I say it. *Someday I'm going to die.*

I sit there awhile in the quiet and then lean back to watch the procession. A couple walks forward carrying their nine-month-old. The pastor marks that baby's head with the same oils and ashes as he marked mine.

I don't like watching them. That sweet baby's head is covered in grime when the couple carries her back to their seats, past my line of vision. I don't want to think of my life and that baby's life on the same plane of time: she will die just as I will.

The ashes aren't just a metaphor for death; they're a metaphor for sin. We recognize our helplessness to save ourselves. We recognize that death is what our broken state has earned us. We recognize how we need a savior.

That baby girl needs a savior too.

The couple is sitting several rows behind me. I don't look back, but I imagine them. I imagine the woman beginning to breastfeed her forehead-smudged daughter. I imagine the baby's innocent gulping of milk. What does she know of heartache and failure? What *will* she know?

Saint Benedict charged his order that in the daily-ness of serving God, we are to remember our own death is coming. It could be today.[4]

Later, I'll hardly recall the sermon preached, the prayers of confession, or even the feeling of being both blessed and marked for death: a cross of ashes streaked across my head. What I will remember in color, in shocking clarity, is that couple and their baby and the thought that my son has entered into this broken world, the thought that my son will die one day too.

10

Mid-February, First Days of Lent

Click-click-click goes the stove. This kitchen is old. The windows don't close all the way. The stovetop is white and black and eighties all over. My twelve-by-twelve inches of counter space are Formica. And in the dark of the long, thin kitchen at nine on a Thursday night, I watch the neighbor drag his trash to the Dumpster outside my window.

I'm in sweats and slippers, and I'm waiting for the cup of tea that will signal to my brain that this day is ending. I listen to the fizz of water heating on the stove. Since we moved here, I've boiled water for this cup of decaf Irish Breakfast tea, added milk, and eaten two squares of dark chocolate (73 percent cocoa) every night. I think I'm becoming a cranky old lady about my two squares of dark chocolate.

Chris is home from traveling. I'm giddy with his return. Before we had August, I used to feel lonely when he was gone. Now I just feel spent. It's not simply that I wish for another grown-up who can have a conversation that's not about sharks in toddler language; it's the sheer weight of feeding and clothing and caring for my little human and never handing the tasks to anyone else. Every day of Chris's absence I feel emotionally weak around five in the evening. I push through those last two-and-a-half hours toward dinner and bedtime and quiet, afraid I won't make it without flopping my body into a mess of a sob on the floor in August's bedroom. Sometimes I end up on the floor; sometimes I don't.

I feel guilty for lamenting my lonesome parenting. How many women in this world are raising children alone right now? How many women in my life are doing it and have done it? Who am I to complain and cry on the floor?

Still, Chris's arrival home tonight was a long, cool drink on a hot day. He and August wrestled on the bed while I made dinner. And after the bath and teeth brushing and book reading and songs sung over the dark crib, Chris and I have plans to snuggle on the couch and watch TV.

It's the first full day of Lent, and even though the water is near steaming on the stove, I'm making the choice to not pull out the nightly dessert. I'm giving it up and replacing it with an Examination of Conscience, the prayer I learned at the monastery. I feel proud of this decision, my being cranky about my dark chocolate and all. Also, I'm excited about the good it might do for my praying life.

Lent is an interesting exercise for those of us who are rule followers. It doesn't take much for humans to turn the purpose of a spiritual practice, in this case a time for inner preparation and renewal prior to Easter, into a rules-based recital. (Were we good enough? Did we give up something hard enough? Was our performance pretty enough?) I know my tendency toward legalism. It's my most natural inclination. I want to do the best thing. I want Jesus to like me most.

The reality is that Jesus did not come up with the idea of Lent. It evolved through centuries of Christians working out their faith as a community. The believers who formed the intricate calendar of the church decided at some point that we faithful needed some good reminders built in to our year. Maybe they knew how much like kids we are, always taking whatever we're given and asking for more. The act of Lent is not about making God happy with us. It is about reminding our souls of something deep and true: We need God more than we need anything else.

∽✍

I loved ministry, and when I began my full-time youth ministry career it felt entirely suited to my personality. Relationships were more important than office work! I could set my own schedule! I could stay in my pajamas at nine in the morning and watch reruns of *Dawson's Creek*! But over time the freedom began to overwhelm me.

My job demanded nights and weekends and large chunks of time away from my husband. Some mentors within the ministry suggested I look at my days as divided into thirds. For one-third of my waking hours, I should rest or be with friends or family. For two-thirds I should work. The difficulty of that concept was my rule-following nature. I like to earn bonus points for Sacrificing The Most.

Soon I felt lost in my daily schedule, constantly adding hours, subtracting them, hoping to do enough. I felt I should work if the sun was up. And I felt extra hard working if I plowed through morning till night, day after day. After all, youth ministry is a goofy job. Anybody who gets to count singing Top 40 hits in the car and cheering at JV soccer games as "work" deserves to keep longer hours.

I went away for weekend and weeklong camps. I was assigned an entire month away each summer while I helped run camp; my husband visited on weekends.

After August was born, I moved to a part-time schedule, which meant I was responsible for direct ministry and less responsible for administration or fund-raising. I could stay at home in the mornings or afternoons with less guilt. But by that point, time had become a heavy burden. I was still working three to four nights a week, but I had changed. Or maybe the weight of the work had changed. I'm not sure which. All I knew was that I was older and wanted to sleep. I wanted to sit on a couch with my husband at the end of the day. I wanted to be off work when he was off work, not eating a hasty meal together before I grabbed my bag and ran out the back door.

Some days I would daydream about what it would look like to sit at home every night of the week. As August moved through his first year of life and I pumped milk for Chris to give him via bottle in the nighttime, I was jealous of every other mother I knew who wasn't pumping at that moment. I was jealous of every person who went to sleep whenever she wanted.

But the jealousy only lasted in my alone moments. When I was speaking to a basement full of high school students on a Thursday night, I was alive. Blood surged in me. I laughed and explained Jesus with boldness—ten minutes after having taken a cream pie in the face. As I dropped a fourteen-year-old off at home, we sat in her driveway and she asked if God could really love her. I stayed up late crying with a girl over her friend's eating disorder. I drove a Suburban full of kids to their friend's funeral following his suicide then sat with them in quiet at the sandwich shop after.

On those nights when I drove home in the eleven o'clock darkness, I begged God to do beautiful things for the fragmented home lives and desperate emotional states of my high school students. I loved my job, but my life felt too heavy-laden with meaning. My emotions swung daily from laughter to sadness, energy to exhaustion. Once I added a baby to the mix, I was sick with the thought of such extremes. I was tired.

Over time, a pastor learns to bear both joy and sorrow, vitality and brokenness, for the people given to her care. She must learn to carry this weight without crushing her own soul. I couldn't hold all that meaning inside me. I was in ministry only four years, hardly long enough to have gained the sort of perspective I might have collected over time.

I wept and pleaded for a path for my exhaustion. I never wanted to stop telling the story of Jesus to insecure sixteen-year-olds. I never wanted to miss watching their faces soften the moment they believed they were loved entirely, completely.

But then I did want to stop. Every day I wanted to stop. Perhaps if I'd stayed in Philadelphia, maturity would have rescued my weariness. Perhaps I would have discovered that my problem was with *time*, not ministry. Time was broken because of my insecurities. But as it was, I could not live up to the rules I'd set for myself. I was near collapse. And then we moved to San Francisco.

∾⸲

Maybe that's why I'm giving up dark chocolate these forty days of Lent. For the past four years, I dreamed of nights spent at home watching TV with Chris or reading together on the couch. I dreamed of the possibility of both of us being present to put our son to bed or take a late evening walk with him in the summer dusk. And here we are: home together at 9 p.m., and I'm already used to the miracle of it.

Maybe the chocolate routine has become a promise of sorts: a promise of rest. I have a nagging sense that my two squares of dark chocolate each night represent something bigger than an emotional need for routine. I have a suspicion that I'm clinging to this ritual because I'm frightened I gave up a sacred calling in order to sit on the couch in my pajamas each night. I am afraid God knows why I like my chocolate. If I release it, God and I might be having Big Conversations I'm too afraid to have. The sooner I remove the chocolate and listen, the sooner I'll move past the fear.

I pour my tea, leave the purple-wrapped candy bar in the fridge, and shuffle down the hallway to my husband on the couch.

Chris is lost in his computer. Nothing came out of his interviews with the start-up, and I'm thankful. I wasn't ready to make another big life decision. I could not have packed up my kid and moved back east without feeling like I didn't try, like I wasn't brave. But at least once a day I still feel weighted by our newness here. I still feel unsteady. This place is not home.

I long for every small thing we left of our lives in Phila-delphia. The friends, the church, the family. But what I miss most is the future we didn't have. That loss rolls into me sometimes in heavy waves from my neck to my belly. Chris and I own a house outside Philadelphia, a house with a cozy blue room we painted when I was pregnant with August. It has a driveway where we pulled up our car in late June, our floppy two-day-old baby in the car seat behind us. It has a little yard and a patio. That patio is where I told my mom and dad I was pregnant. That patio is where August sat outside in the early spring chilled air in his navy sweatshirt and smiled a grin I thought might shatter me.

The future that never happened. That's what I miss. The continuation of friendships, the plans I'd made for nature walks through the trail down the block. I was going to show August how to grab a roly-poly bug and let it tickle across his hand. We were going to sing songs, learn colors, watch the birds, and tell long stories about rockets in that little yard. We were going to grow up there, that boy and me. And our whole family—Chris and August and the children I dreamed would come—would watch the baby maple grow. We would walk to the ice cream shop on warm summer nights. August would learn to ride his bike in the driveway.

Look at us. What am I doing in this tiny apartment, sticking quarters in the shared laundry machines one courtyard and two staircases from my back door, when I own (I own!) a washer and dryer in a basement three thousand miles and three time zones away from here? What am I doing walking with my son through rain puddles in Washington Square Park, trying to learn which of the five homeless men on the park benches is trustworthy and which might scream obscenities at my toddler? I'm trying here. I want to love it here. I do. I think I do. But here, right now, sitting on the couch beside this man I love, I cannot take in my breath. So much has been lost. All of my plans have been lost. What were we thinking?

And now I don't even have any chocolate to eat.

I bring my teacup to my lips. I purse and blow. How did giving up chocolate lead me to this panic? It had something to do with what I think I deserve. What I want. What I use to satisfy the deep longing in me.

It was something about how I was going to pray instead.

11

Early March, Second Week of Lent

It's the second week of Lent, and I still haven't succumbed to the dark chocolate. What has been a lot more difficult is the nighttime prayer practice I was hoping to have put in place. Night prayer is difficult because I'm so tired; once I finally sit down in the evening I can't bear to use my brain. It's a lot easier to skip the chocolate and go straight to bed.

Sometimes I give up. Most of the time I give up. But some nights, especially this past week, I've been able to steer my mind straight into the Examination of Conscience right before (or in spite of) the comfort of my covers.

When I practice this sort of prayer, I start by reminding myself of God's presence. Then I look through my day with gratitude and review it in light of my actions and my heart. How was my heart divided? How was I loving? How was I broken? How did I break others? The prayer concludes by imagining Jesus taking a seat beside me. I talk these things out with him.

Of course, being under the covers in my pajamas doesn't help my prayer life. I don't usually make it through the second step. But tonight I'm in my bed, my head propped up on two pillows, and I'm alert long enough to consider all the goodness.

I begin with the morning: the way August's hair stuck up in front when he woke. The way he and I laughed when his head got stuck in the neck hole of his shirt while I dressed him. I list the conversation with the nice mom at the park. I list my afternoon time of quiet during August's nap and the chance to open a book. I thank God for clean diapers and water and even the quarter-slotted laundry machines. I list and I list. I think of Chris's face with two-day stubble. I think of my ever-improving attempts at pork chops. I think of bedtime rituals and August's tiny bedroom.

And then I fall asleep.

PART 3

Prime: Second Morning Prayer

Returning to the work of God.
Repetition.

Always we begin again.

—The Rule of Saint Benedict

12

Late March, Fifth Week of Lent

August rides his tricycle toward the intersection at Columbus and Stockton, though *rides* might be a generous term. He's strapped into the red plastic seat, and I push him along from the extended handle at the back. His toes hang and drag onto the pavement, but he holds the handlebars as if he's a professional. His grip is fierce, his eyes intense. The scene makes the elderly Chinese woman and her daughter giggle and pat his helmet-clad head as they pass us in the crosswalk. I manage a weak smile and try to imagine what they're saying to one another in Cantonese. I woke up sad this morning and am doing everything I can to rise out of the muck in my head.

Deep breath. Okay, my child is a gift. My life is a gift.

Today I'm going to be grateful. I'm going to take steps toward joy. I stare at the buildings and people we pass, thanking God for them, asking God to show me how to love this city. The thought of San Francisco drags me out of my thirty seconds of thanksgiving. Do I even like this place? Maybe this move has shaken me too deeply. I've been clinically depressed before. I'm afraid to go back.

"Micha!" I turn my head to see Kristen and Amelia walking toward us from the coffee shop on Stockton. Amelia's in her stroller, holding a tiny cup of steamed milk. Kristen waves.

"I thought that was you!" she says. "How are you?"

How am I? I turn August's tricycle around to face our friends. The kids look at each other from their respective seats. I'm fine. I'm good, right?

"Good. Just heading to the bank. What are you guys up to?" I smile.

"Gladys is coming to watch Amelia in ten minutes so we're just heading back from our coffee date. I have to work this afternoon." She leans down to August. "Hey, buddy! Are you riding a tricycle?"

August smiles at her. "My hat." He hits his helmet.

"It's a cool hat, August."

She stands up. "Oh, I've been meaning to ask, have you heard about the neighborhood Easter egg hunt?"

"No . . ."

"It's for all the kids in North Beach. A ton of people come out for it every year. It's really cute."

"So sweet. I love that."

"Yeah. You guys should come. I think it's Saturday morning before Easter, but I can't remember what time it starts. I'll find out, okay? I'll let you know."

"Yeah. Sounds great."

She looks at her phone. "Oh! Gotta run. See you later?"

"For sure." I smile and lean over to my boy. "Aug, can you say bye to Amelia?"

He stares at Amelia, and she stares back. They have nothing to add to this conversation. I laugh and shrug at Kristen. "See you later."

This brief exchange, these two minutes of seeing a friend on the sidewalk, is enough to shake me out of my angst for a moment. *I do have friends here,* I think. *I'm not alone here.* I look back at the other people walking sidewalks and passing by my son and me. We're standing on a sidewalk in the middle of North Beach, and all of these people live here. With us. We live here. This is our home.

I need to live like this is my home.

The Benedictines take three vows when they offer themselves to the monastic life: obedience (to the rule and to the abbot, or leader, of their monastery), *conversatio moralis*, sometimes understood as "conversion of life," and stability. Every instruction in Benedict's Rule flows out of these three commitments.[1]

That vow to stability is the thing that sets Benedictines apart from every other monastic order, something I didn't know when I first began to study Benedict's Rule. It's a concept that feels countercultural. After all, I am from a generation that values change above all else: technology and careers should always be evolving. We transform in order to remain necessary. If we don't change, we're left behind.

When a monk makes a vow to stability, he is not committing to a general spiritual concept; he is vowing to remain in a single place, with a single group of people, for an entire lifetime. The monastery is his lifelong home, the monks and nuns his family. For better or worse.

Maybe Saint Benedict chose stability in response to his own choices. After all, his story starts with a teenage boy leaving everything to follow Jesus. Changing his home and his lifestyle and his future for the sake of his God. Did those three years in the cave at Subiaco teach him to grow weary of the human desire to find something more interesting, more challenging, or more demanding?

Leaving often masquerades as the more courageous choice. But in reality it's often easier to leave a relationship than to pursue it despite the difficulty. Stability demands forgiveness, discomfort and, often, a sacrifice of the more interesting, more exciting possibility. Stability is brave.

Maybe courage is what I'm missing. I don't want to put down roots here in this city. I don't want to make any vows right now. I want to get out. I want to tuck my husband and baby into a cart and drag us from this place. I don't know where I want to go, but I need to go somewhere. I need to go home. I just don't know where that is.

The first night Chris mentioned the possibly of our moving away from Philadelphia, it was December. We were lying in bed, and August was asleep down the hall. I was overwhelmed with ministry and my ever-more-demanding six-month-old. I was worried that if I settled down in Pennsylvania, I'd never live near my family in Texas again. I was worried I wouldn't be there in my parents' old age. I was worried my family would always feel I'd betrayed them.

So when Chris said, "There's this opportunity . . ." When he said, "Would you ever consider this?" My first thought was not of the ministry to which I'd given the past four years or of the friends and family in Philadelphia who loved us and our son. It was a thought of relief: that I wouldn't have to hold the guilt anymore. I could live far from my family in Texas and Chris's family on the East Coast, and somehow breaking *everyone's* heart would be easier than breaking just a few.

August is singing to himself, a toddler-mumble song. I park his tricycle next to me as we arrive at the red-brick bank building. He stares out at the mass of people moving past us. We're a block from Chinatown. Down the street a man in a white butcher apron carries a whole pig carcass on his back, each of his hands grasping a pig hoof while the animal's lifeless corpse hangs snout-down against his back.

So many worlds in one place.

My left hand covers my right as it punches the passcode into the sidewalk ATM. I place the cash into my wallet, drop the wallet into my bag. I maneuver the tricycle around and turn back toward home.

Have I been discontent? Lonely? Maybe this move has jostled something loose in me: the thing that makes me grateful, or brave, or open to people, or kind to myself.

Maybe I'm broken, I think. Maybe I simply can't commit to stability because I can't commit to this moment, right now. Jean-Pierre de Caussade, an eighteenth-century French Jesuit, wrote that Christ comes to us in a fresh way every moment, every day. We don't have to separate the secular from the sacred. Christ is alive right now, in all of it.

"Precious moment," de Caussade wrote, "how small in the eyes of my head and how great in those of my heart, the means whereby I receive small things from the Father who reigns in heaven! Everything that falls from there is very excellent, every-thing bears the mark of its maker."[2]

All of the mundane is "excellent." All of it "bears the mark of its maker." Is that possible? How would I live if I believed that?

I came to Benedict's Rule because I longed for enough time to be who I wanted to be, but I'm not really sure what that means. I've been wondering if, underneath that fear of time, I was longing for someone to tell me that the ordinary is good, that making dinner and picking up the house and reading ABC books takes courage. Can I believe that God loves the ordinary? That God loves the ordinary in me?

I've spent so much of my life valuing the radical above the ordinary. The most important jobs were the ones with eternal significance. The most important tasks were spiritual. Every-thing else held less value. As long as I was in ministry, I was safe. But what about now? Now I'm simple. I'm just another mom.

Another woman at the ATM on a Tuesday afternoon, heading home to fold laundry and take out the trash. I have a deep-rooted fear that God is simply the Trophy-Giver, conferring honors on the hardest workers, on those most deserving of love. And I'm not doing enough to deserve anything.

I pass the homeless woman who always sits on the corner of Stockton and Columbus. She is old, with deep eyes, and she stares straight through me every time I pass her. Always on this corner.

"Ma'am," I ask, "do you need anything to eat?"

She doesn't answer. I stand there for a moment with my little boy beside me, looking, waiting. She doesn't meet my eyes. "Okay," I say. "Take care."

I walk on, unsure of myself. Unsure of what Jesus would do here in this city, if Jesus were a mom at Stockton and Columbus, pushing her son in a tricycle.

"Jesus," I whisper as I cross Columbus and head north. I pray the name as if that name might encapsulate all my prayers. Maybe "Jesus" is the only prayer I'm ever praying, whether I'm longing for the vacant-eyed woman to be gathered and fed or searching for wisdom to know how to do the gathering and feeding.

"Jesus," I pray for myself and this darkness in me, this hope that one day I might be free of it. "Jesus," I pray, in thanksgiving, for my boy in his red helmet and for my friend on the sidewalk and the hope that this may be home one day because I see the butcher and the pig carcass and the old woman shuffling across the street, her arm hooked into her daughter's. I see the beautiful colors of all these shops and all these people, and I might love them. I think I do. *Jesus.*

13

Late March, Fifth Week of Lent

"Oh, Lord, open my lips, and my mouth will declare your praise," I whisper with all the Benedictines around this world this morning. I pray the words in the kitchen while I measure out coffee grounds and pour water into the pot. I let my sleepy eyes draw an invisible line around myself on the terra-cotta tiles, a quiet circle of light in the darkness of the morning.

I join with all the monks up before sunrise. We practice Lauds, prayer "at the first light of daybreak," as Benedict instructs. And the first words the monks are to utter are these, this phrase from Psalm 51: "Open my lips, and my mouth will declare your praise."[1] I like that these small words are a gathering prayer, a prayer for not only entering God's presence but entering a new day.

The more I study Saint Benedict's Rule, the more I imagine I'm becoming friends with the saint himself. I want to understand him. What shaped his theology? Why did he choose this Psalm, of all of them, to recite when the sun lifted out of earth's dark pocket each morning?

He's still just a shadow, though, half superhero, half grandfather. And I can't seem to read enough to lift Benedict from the mysterious haze. In *Life and Miracles of Saint Benedict*, a biographical pamphlet of sorts written by Saint Gregory in AD 593, Benedict appears shrouded in eternal light at all times. When he isn't miraculously retrieving sharp instruments from the bottom of lakes or convincing a raven to fly away with the poisoned bread sent from a jealous priest, Benedict seems lonely: always teaching, never laughing.[2]

Granted, Saint Gregory, who was pope at that time, was not trying to write a biography in the modern sense of the word.

In *Man of Blessing: A Life of Saint Benedict*, Carmen Acevedo Butcher explains that Gregory didn't "set out to write a chronological, historically anchored story" of Benedict's life. Instead his goal was to prove Benedict's holiness, to elevate the abbot, who'd been dead for forty years by then, to the glories of sainthood.[3]

As a faulty believer who is most drawn to Saint Benedict's genuine understanding of human frailty, I read the semi-historical book with longing for the real Benedict to arrive and roll his eyes, beg us to ignore the wild stories being told of him. It's not that I doubt God used Benedict to accomplish miraculous things. It's simply the way they're told, as if Benedict had been supplied with a genetic mutation that allowed him to live above every dark thought, every physical longing, while simultaneously performing supernatural feats once a week. Gregory's book leaves me wishing for any hint, any revelation at all, that Benedict was actually human.

The coffee drips from the funnel into the glass pitcher, and I turn my mind back to prayer. I retrieve my Bible from the next room and return to stand beside the coffeepot. I open the pages to Psalm 22 and whisper the words aloud.

The psalmist starts this one angry. "Why have you forsaken me?"[4] He begs for an answer to his disappointment in God. I understand that kind of disappointment: The dark, secret worry that maybe the God you love doesn't really love you. Or maybe the God you love isn't even real at all.

I pray the words. They unsettle me. Then there's a turnaround, a conversion from anger to trust. What changes for the speaker? How does he move from disgust with God to, "You are my strength; come quickly to help me"?[5]

The coffee stops dripping. I pull out my mug and fill it. I tend to label doubt and belief as opposites. If I doubt God's goodness I tell myself I'm a disaster, and if I feel God's presence I sigh my relief. But part of what draws me to Saint Benedict's Rule is the possibility that there is room for both at the same time: the doubt *and* the belief, the disappointment *and* the acceptance.

I take my coffee to the living room, click on the lamp. Of course, that's why I've been so annoyed with Gregory's version of Benedict. I was hoping for a Benedict who could hold all our complexities. I don't want a saint. I want a psalmist.

In eleventh grade the traveling revival preacher stood before our congregation and insisted that if we trusted Jesus enough, we could go an entire day without sin, without dark thoughts, without hurting another person or displeasing God. He wasn't your typical traveling evangelist: He was tall and skinny and young, not the bulbous, sweat-drenched, fist-pounding type. He didn't raise his voice. He was earnest and sincere as he preached night after night in our two-week-long revival series.

We were drawn to his charisma. He would punctuate his syllables so quick it made our hearts pound hard against our rib bones. Then he'd turn the volume down so the congregation would lean forward, the hair lifting on our arms, all of us longing for resolution, for good news. We wanted a life without sin. We wanted to be healed.

Revivals were nothing new to me. In my Southern Baptist childhood, they came twice a year and usually demanded an entire week of my family's life. We'd have church every night, rushing through our afternoons, trying to get homework done so we could be in the sanctuary by 7 p.m. I didn't mind that part.

I loved my church. The community served as almost another home, another parent even, in my life. What I dreaded was the requirements of revivals: We were supposed to bring friends, the unspiritual in particular. We were supposed to pack the pews with those who needed to hear the message of salvation. The fuller the sanctuary, the more we were praised for our faithfulness to God.

I knew, though, by the time I was sixteen, that the message of salvation I wanted my friends to experience was different from the loud words they'd hear from the mouth of most revival preachers. I didn't trust the sermons. There was too much hell, too much fear, too much rhetorical manipulation. My sixteen-year-old self could never have explained the reasons I wasn't comfortable. In fact, I carried guilt that I wasn't bold enough to bring my friends. I assumed I was too afraid to tell them about Jesus. I didn't value their salvation enough. The reality, though, was a deeper discomfort. I knew something was not right about what my church was doing all those nights as the revival preacher paced the stage. My psyche told me to be wary. I listened.

That night the seven-hundred-seat sanctuary was packed full, so full that I stood with my friends in the far left aisle, beside the stained glass image of the orange bread and the blood red cup set out on a blue table. The evangelist had been moving through the story of the cross, night after night. His interpretation was nothing too new: Christ had died on the cross. Christ had risen. And we had to get ourselves right. We had to receive the gift of eternal life. Had we? Had we submitted to God? Had we given everything over? Had we prayed the Sinner's Prayer, begged God's intervention on our souls' behalf?[6] Would we die without salvation?

But that night the preacher changed things up. This was a sermon for the believers in the room, the ones already en route to heaven. He was convinced the sanctuary was packed full of people who had trusted Jesus for salvation but weren't living changed lives. We were just like everyone else in the world, moving through each day unaware of God's presence: entertaining, feeding, enjoying ourselves while the world around us burned. Our self-obsession was sin. We were rebellious people who had once hoped to follow God into the dark world but instead had become trapped by its pleasures: sex, drink, faithlessness. We were sinners.

That's when he said it, with the traveling chorus on the stage beside him. They were humming a hymn, all dressed in red, and smiling. They heard this sermon every week. They knew the zinger that was coming.

"My friends . . ." He left the pulpit and walked to the middle of the stage so he could lean in close, telling us a story we would not believe unless we heard it that night, unless we listened hard enough this very moment. "You know what's true about you in the darkness. You know the secrets you keep from the people around you. You don't hide God's Word in your heart. You're content to value work and family and your own comfort over the message of the gospel. You are clean on the outside, but inside you're full of dead men's bones.

"I'm here tonight to tell you . . ." He leaned in close and lowered his voice to a whisper. "You are not a slave to sin. You don't *have* to sin!"

"Did you hear me?" He laughed, turning to his traveling chorus on the stage beside him. They laughed with him. "You don't have to sin!"

We shifted in our seats. A few "Amens" came from the men in the audience, waiting for more. He walked back to his notes on the lectern. "Do you think you could go an entire day without one evil thought, without lusting for another woman besides your wife, men? Without joining in the gossip, ladies? Without watching the filth on television?

"You don't have to sin!" He started pacing again, moving toward the other side of the room, where I stood, so he could look in our eyes. "Do you believe that? Do you believe you can *choose* to make it through one day without sneaking that whiskey you've hidden in the closet?"

He turned his face and raised his eyebrow, "Yes, brother," he said, peering out into the audience, "I know about you and the secret bottle in the closet. You're spending your life pretending you're a good Christian man, but I know what you're doing behind closed doors. God *knows* what you're doing behind closed doors."

"Amen," came some deep voices, echoing around the room.

"You are not a *slave* again to sin, church!" the preacher said, setting his hand carefully on the pulpit. He quieted again. "I'm here today to whisper the truth: you can go a day without sin.

"I know you can because I have. Because I do."

We all sighed. Did he just say that? Did he just say it's possible for a human to make it through twenty-four hours having never acted out of selfishness or vanity or jealousy, without speaking words we regret?

The singers nodded their heads in agreement. *Yes! We can live without sin!* their bright faces said.

I felt a thud in my spirit and something like lead dropped onto my chest. My breath shortened, and I asked God what was wrong here. I wanted to believe the preacher. I knew I was a sinner. I knew I was supposed to be a better witness for Jesus. But these words, this sermon, did not free me. The words squeezed my insides. They felt wrong.

It wasn't that I thought the preacher was lying. I hadn't yet come to distrust spiritual leaders in my world. I didn't yet know about ministers who lie or pretend or abuse people. What I felt that moment was fear. I stood beside the stained glass, staring out into my congregation, all those people I loved, and I was afraid.

Is this it? Sinlessness? I asked myself. *Did God really create us just so we would* not *screw up? Is this preacher really living the full life Jesus says we can live?* Despite all my naiveté, despite my longing to be a good girl, I looked hard at that skinny man in a suit on the stage, and I didn't believe.

But something deeper was moving in me than disbelief. I didn't *want* to believe him. I didn't *want* his faith of buffed-up piety.

I looked around the room at the adults who had rocked me as a baby, who had taught my Sunday school classes and served as deacons and helped pay my way to youth camp each summer. They were being lied to. And someone needed to speak up and tell the truth. Someone needed to lift the lead from our chests.

Can you try so hard to be perfect that you miss God? I wondered. *Maybe they're missing God.*

I took deep breaths and picked at my fingernails. I moved my eyes from stage to congregation, congregation to stage, waiting for something to happen. Surely everyone around me was thinking the same thing. Surely someone else was looking for life but only finding death in this man's words. *Maybe the preacher doesn't even know he's getting the whole story wrong.* But what was the whole story? What was Jesus really offering me when he washed me clean and settled in my spirit?

I waited, but no one stood up. No one said, "Brother, Jesus has something even more beautiful than sinlessness." No one came to my rescue. I saw heads nod. I heard more hearty "Amens" from the deacons in their seats.

Yes, Jesus had something more for us. I knew it. I just wasn't sure what it was. So I tried to ignore that feeling. I prayed God might let me also go a day without gossiping about a friend or rolling my eyes when a teacher expected an obscene amount of essay writing. I prayed that I might be able to forgive totally, all at once, the wrong my recently exed boyfriend had committed behind my back with my long-legged blonde friend.

What came slow and fierce into my gut that night, as I stood beside the stained glass, the sun already sunk deep into the earth outside the windows, was not a release from my guilt and not even a confirmation that I was right about the crushing spirit I'd felt sliver into the people around me. What came was a vision of sin: It was not something I could just stop. It was not simple wrongdoing. It was deeper. It was brokenness. It was *in* me more than it was coming out of me. My spirit was tilted, imbalanced. I was off kilter deep in the unknown places, and *that* was what needed fixing. And, even more, this was the case for the whole world. We were all askew, all looking for something to right us, to set us toward True North.

Maybe following Jesus was much more complex and much more simple than all this sin control. Maybe if I found the simplicity I'd understand the complexity. I'd discover the *abundant life* Jesus was always talking about.

FOUND

The preacher asked us to come forward, to come confess our sins, receive the Holy Spirit, and change our lives. I stood still, my back pressed heavy into the window.

☙❧

When I read Saint Benedict's Rule, I find space there for imperfect people, hope for those people like me who never quite live up. Benedict, even in AD 500, was capable of recognizing that humans can be bold and faithful yet inconsistent and troubled in our deepest places. We can care for and honor the people in need around us and still crawl in despair after recognition and self-obsession. We can live self-sacrificially and generously yet be motivated by a dark need for approval. We can know God and still do terrible things to one another.

Despite the few moments in the rule in which Benedict prescribes striking or whipping for disobedience,[7] he was surprisingly capable of moving beyond his culture's norms in the practical ways he made room for human weakness within the monastery.[8] He gave jobs to the physically weak and the mentally weak, those his culture had rejected. He set standards in order to help those who struggled with taking "too much wine." He knew that gossip is sometimes hard to avoid, so he made meals a time for quiet. He knew that early morning prayer is difficult, so he encouraged his brothers to help each other out of bed. He called prayer "the work of God," perhaps because he knew it *is* work.

Unless we recognize our own sin, unless we become intimately familiar with our own brokenness, we cannot offer the kind of hope Saint Benedict gave his monks. Only those who acknowledge their own weakness can extend mercy to the weak world around them. Maybe the people closest to whole are those most aware of how fractured they actually are.

Here in my living room, once again on the couch with coffee in my hands, I feel a gentle reassurance that God holds more for me than a rules-obsessed faith. I feel God's hand scoop a small cavern in my chest. Into that hollow spot, God pours grace. Grace for my confusion, for my self-anger, for my wild doubt. I feel God fill that hollow space in my chest, and I sigh.

The Lord knows how I am tilted. God knows I am just like the weakest of the monks. I'm the one who can hardly get out of bed. I'm the one who begs to believe but fails again and again. I'm the one who judges and scoffs and forgets the work of God. And there, between my ribs, in the empty God-scooped place, I invite Jesus, the champion of the weak-willed and beaten-down, to make me whole.

Oh, Lord, open my lips and my mouth will declare your praise.

14

Early April, Holy Week

For the years since I've been following the church calendar and moving through Lent, I'm always a bit intimidated once the week before Easter comes along. There's some inexplicable pressure for me in these days leading up to the cross. Maybe it's my inner-evangelical youth group girl who fully expects an emotional come-to-Jesus moment on Thursday night of youth camp. Am I hoping all these weeks of chocolate-free evenings will culminate in a sudden clear connection to God? Will I suddenly feel God speak to me the way I once did? And if I don't, is it because I've failed to listen? Because I've hardened?

There's also this: my mother-in-law arrives tomorrow, and the windows are smudged with toddler mouth marks, the bathroom mirror covered in white toothpaste splats. Before I can have any sort of dramatic Holy Week epiphanies, I need to scrub.

೨~ಲ

It's Holy Wednesday, and August and I make sugar cookies. I roll out the dough, and he pounds it, half singing, half shouting, "Cookie! Cookie! Cookie!" over and over.

He takes a lump of dough and presses his finger into it. Poke. Poke. Poke. I think of Doubting Thomas as I watch August's chubby fingers press in and out of the dough. All week, Caravaggio's painting *The Incredulity of Saint Thomas* has been on my mind. That painting makes me nervous. In it, Thomas encounters the resurrected Christ face to face, and that pallor-skinned Jesus offers his torn side, peeling back the flesh. Thomas sticks his finger all the way inside.

Of all the Easter stories, of all the followers of Jesus who encounter the resurrected Christ, it's Thomas's response that makes the most sense to me. I know if I had been among the disciples, I would have been the one doubting Mary Magdalene's big tale of an empty tomb. I would have been the scoffer. The difference between Thomas and me is that I would have done my best to tidy up that disbelief. I would have been a lot more polite about it.

I like Thomas for his bravery, for his willingness to demand something from his friend Jesus. And I love Jesus for giving him exactly what he needed. Thomas wanted physical proof. Jesus let Thomas stick his hand into the open wound.

Caravaggio's scene is grotesque and dark. But at the same time, Thomas's lips are pursed in some comedic *Oh!*, the same surprised expression I saw on the cartoon train yesterday in

August's *Thomas the Tank Engine* video. And somehow, even that over-the-top exclamation works for me. Who am I to judge what my reaction would be if I had my pointer finger pushed through my Savior's skin? The painting forces me to recognize not only Christ's suffering in Thomas's skepticism but also Christ's refusal to demand belief. Jesus is kind to his friend, even after everyone else around Thomas has offered a healthier faith. Of all Christ's followers, only Thomas demands more of his teacher.

I understand why. I understand the urgency of doubt, the longing to straighten the wrinkles out in my mind, make every connection from God to humanity linear. I long for an answer to every biblical uncertainty. I want to hold a deep conviction so I can explain away those Scripture passages that make me squirm.

When I find Thomas's story of doubt and belief in the Gospel of John, I find my story too. I'm not outside the room of believers. I'm here praying and sometimes hiding, waiting for Jesus to appear and do something fierce. But I hesitate when everyone else goes on and on. "We have seen the Lord," they say.[1]

Usually, I stay quiet, contemplating the possibility of their words, asking God to help me believe. But sometimes I'm bold with Thomas: "Unless I see in his hands the mark of the nails, and place my finger into the mark of the nails, and place my hand into his side, I will never believe."[2]

When his new resurrected body appears to his followers in that closed-off room, Jesus essentially says this: *Believe or don't believe, Thomas. Only experience me first before you make your choice.*

What I have come to embrace about my own skepticism is that it forces me into that same daily choice. My pastor said this once: "Of Jesus you can either say, 'He is of no value,' or 'He is of ultimate value.' You can't say, 'He is of *some* value.'"

There's no room for moderation in the resurrection story. Either it happened or it didn't. Either Thomas put his hand into Christ's side or Jesus' bones are lying in a cave somewhere. Either this is the wildest story ever told—God becomes a human, loses his life and overcomes death for our sake, and makes bold promises about the future of the world, its restoration, our complete healing and renewal—or Jesus was simply a wise man with an irrational lying streak whose unhinged followers were willing to go to the lions before they would admit they'd made up the whole thing.

Christ's resurrection makes him vulnerable. He is vulnerable to our doubt and vulnerable to our fingers forced through his wounded skin. He knows we need to be reminded that his love for us extends into our fears and broken places. And for me that means being brave enough to approach him and ask for the reminder.

I take August's mashed up slab of dough, sprinkle flour on it and roll it out. "Cookie!" he shouts as I hand him the flat, smooth shape of dough and he sets it haphazardly beside the others.

15

Early April, Good Friday

I walk with an umbrella to our car parked a few blocks away and then swing by the house to pick up my mother-in-law and August, who are waiting on the front porch. It's raining and cold, and by the time I pull into the neighbor's driveway and throw on the hazards, it's already 11:40. The service is at noon. As usual, I am proving myself incapable of making it anywhere on time. Just once, I'd like to appear responsible in the presence of my mother-in-law, who never has any trouble arriving early. Unless, of course, she's riding with me.

For the past few years I've prayed through the Stations of the Cross on Good Friday. My friend Anna painted a series for the stations, and our former church outside Philadelphia has displayed them for the past several years during Holy Week. Last year, when August was nine or ten months old, I left the house while he and Chris were still sleeping and kept vigil at 6 a.m. with those paintings. I prayed alone in that big stone sanctuary and walked from image to image, remembering the event of Christ's death as if I were part of it. Which I guess I was.

I'm missing that today.

It's been raining and cold for weeks, it seems. I'm bone-chilled and grumpy, convinced that I will never see the sun again unless I move out of this town. A Syracuse friend always said Good Friday should be cold and rainy. I like that idea. I guess a sunny, warm Good Friday is suspect. But I'm still a little edgy, wishing for a real spring to show up and prove that San Francisco is as great as everybody says it is.

My mother-in-law got in last night, and Chris is at work today. Her visit has sparked anxiety in my belly. I want her to be happy and comfortable. I want her to think I'm doing a good job, that I'm a good mom, that our home is a place with joy in it. Barb's sleeping on a blow-up mattress on the living room floor next to the old window that doesn't close all the way. It whistles a breeze into the room while that loose manhole cover clangs outside. There's not a heating vent near her, and we only own two extra blankets. I think we might not be abounding in hospitality.

Of course, just as my mother taught me, I washed everything I could wash before Barb arrived. I stocked the fridge with food she likes: Diet Coke and bagels and beer and romaine lettuce. August has been wild with excitement for her arrival. As long as I've been in love with her son, Barb and I have spent Good Friday together. When Chris and I lived nearby, Barb and I would meet at a noontime Good Friday service and then hit up a cheese farm for samples. (Our tradition is far from fasting, I know.) It feels right to have her here today, even though I know traveling is not her favorite thing and neither is the cold and rain.

I sit through the service asking God to remind me of whatever I need to see, whatever I'm too distracted to notice. A man with a deep voice and scruffy beard reads the entire crucifixion story, and I try not to push myself to feel anything. I just sit with the words. My eyes are closed, and the man's deep bass rumbles like the voice of God. So when we get to Jesus' wail—"My God! My God! Why have you forsaken me?"—I sigh a knowing breath.[1]

In the same way you can't understand spring without the winter suffering, the warm thaw of Easter cannot be celebrated without first sinking into the cold, dark murk of Good Friday. That's why I need liturgy in my life. That's why I need a church calendar to guide me into sadness or celebration.

I need permission to be dunked into the deep. And I need liturgy's tether to yank me back up to the surface so I don't drown. The spiritual life is never just a forward climb. It is more of a plunging breathlessly under the waters and a being rescued again and again.

My God, my God. Why have you forsaken me? I whisper it in the moment of silence. And I have the grace to think, *There's hope just in knowing that God can hold my lament.* Even in his darkest moment, Jesus has faith enough to offer God his hard question.

Barb and I leave the worship space in silence and gather August from childcare. We unfold his stroller at the door, pop our umbrellas, and step out into the weeping afternoon. We walk quietly the four blocks to our car, then drive to Fillmore Street and find a spot in a cozy, warm café with dark wood benches and people playing checkers in the corner. Barb has a salad. I eat tomato soup and tear bits of a grilled cheese sandwich off to set before my boy.

Saint Benedict instructed his brothers to "keep the reality of death always before [their] eyes."[2] It's been a slow transition to move from a life of faith without the church calendar to a life of faith within it. But these last few years I've been learning to give my days over to the liturgy. To spend a day focused on death and grief is far from natural. In fact, after the service, Barb and I catch up like we're sharing any other lunch on any other rainy day. We talk about the women I've been getting to know through the Moms' Group at church. I tell her about how hard it is to live in this city. I whine a little over the burden of raising a child without a backyard and the harshness of my daily hunt for parking.

After lunch, we drive to Costco to pick up food for our Easter feast. We sample the cheese cubes there, though compared to the raw-cheese farm in Bucks County, they're a little lacking.

Is there really a way to keep death always before your eyes in the middle of living and working and washing the dishes and forcing your kids to brush their teeth? How are we really supposed to practice Good Friday?

Later, I'll find this tenth-century Celtic prayer:

Christ's Cross over this face, and thus over my ear. Christ's Cross over these eyes . . . this mouth . . . this throat . . . the back of this head . . . this side . . . to accompany before me . . . to accompany behind me . . . Christ's Cross to meet every difficulty both on hollow and on hill . . . Christ's Cross over my community. Christ's Cross over my church. Christ's Cross in the next world. Christ's Cross in this world.[3]

Christ's Cross in this world. This world where I live my daily life and complain about parking and slurp tomato soup and consume as many chips and salsa samples as the Costco employees will give me.

We pack oversized bundles of lettuce and hummus into the car, and I drive us home. August slips into his afternoon sleep as the car creeps closer to North Beach. I pull up beside our flat, turn the flashers on, and carry August through the rain, up the stairs, and into bed. Barb seems tired. I leave her with her book, shut the front door, and splash across the sidewalk to my car, and then wander the streets for any open parking.

Five minutes later, I back into a spot that overlooks the gray water of the bay. Gray goes on for ages out there. Gray sky hovering over gray sea, colliding into a gray bridge where tiny vehicles speed across it. Everything is horizontal. Everything expands past my vision point. I open the car door, snap my umbrella into place, and stand on the sidewalk gazing over the water, everything wet spilling off the edges into gray.

16

Early April, Easter Sunday

I've been standing beside my husband every Easter since we met. I stood beside him when the trumpeted processional began at the Episcopal church of his childhood, when the priests burst through the doors and we all felt our ribs expand against our skin to hold the drama and the boldness of the words we sang: "Christ the Lord is risen today!"[1] And, above our heads, carried high by the long-legged, pimply acolyte, was the shining golden cross bouncing through air, empty and beautiful.

This year we spend Easter with our San Francisco church. City Church doesn't have a building. We meet in the Russian Center, where a czar's crest hangs over our pastor's head and the disco ball meant for the Russian community's annual Vodka Festival remains permanently fixed above the congregation. Here we keep the liturgy, but with a lot less pomp. No acolyte. No horns or loud choir. No priests in robes. But still, as the regular band and the string quartet lead us into our first song of Easter Sunday, I peek over at my husband and smile. Chris can never make it through that first Easter hymn without tears.

When I met Chris I was a poetry student, newly planted in the "godless" Northeast, struggling between my longing for the ease and simplicity of evangelical West Texas and the freedom of life outside of that cultural boundary. I wavered between the naiveté of my good-girl Baptist ideals and the longing I carried for a middle space, where my tendency toward mystery and uncertainty could find a home in my faith.

Much of my spiritual formation had been focused toward turning faith to action, into *holiness*. I still had that revival preacher's voice in my head, even though I didn't trust him. I wanted my faith to turn some other direction. But until I could figure out what that meant, I clung tightly to the spiritual work of perfecting myself.

Chris's faith was different. He had no baggage of guilt or fear, and he believed with a sort of confidence I'd never really seen before. He fascinated and bothered me. Why was he so unconcerned with everyone else's approval? He was always game for a long theological discussion. He knew the Bible and was passionate about it. But I worried he wasn't outwardly "Christian" enough. I'd come from a college of Texan boys who knew how to wax eloquent on all things Jesus. They were ministry boys, future pastors. They carried tiny Bibles in their back pockets. Chris didn't even take his Bible to church.

Once when we were first dating, he left for the bathroom, and I snuck a peek at the Bible he kept by his bed. Not a word was underlined. Mine, of course, was a mess of wiggly lines and exclamation points and hearts in the margins. I couldn't make sense of him.

But I was drawn to his faith. It felt weightier, richer. I was keeping stock of his spiritual fiber, though, and his was not as smooth as I would have preferred. When he cursed as we got lost on the way to meet his grandparents in Princeton, I made a mental note. When he seemed to know way more about Scotch than I thought Christians were allowed to know, I added the problem to my unwritten list. And when he wore clothes from fancy stores that I thought Christians shouldn't shop at (cheaper being more godly, in order to give more money away) I wondered, *What does it mean to be wholly committed to following Jesus?* Maybe it looked different than I always thought.

I would never have used the phrase *spiritual courage* then, but I was looking for it. I wanted someone to be honest with me about the difficulty of faith, to confess the fears everyone else was afraid to say. I wanted Doubting Thomas to notice me standing in the corner among the believers, smiling despite the skepticism that boiled under my surface. I wanted him to grab my hand and say, "She doesn't know the answer either!"

Chris and I spent those first few months of our dating lives doing the thing we'd keep doing long into our marriage: reminding each other why we believed in Jesus. Chris understood what I meant when I said life was both beautiful and an unbearable mess most of the time. He understood when I found courage in the most secret moments, our bodies side by side in the grass under the stars, to say I didn't know if God was real.

He opened a door for me into a room for the imperfect seekers. I had always belonged there. Over time, my darkest questions had woven themselves into my daily experience of God. I believed and I struggled to believe, always, at the same time. Chris simply showed me that it was possible to hold both; it was possible to be imperfect and still be loved.

☙❧

We stand in the back of the Russian Center. "Come and see, Look on this mystery," we sing.[2] So often my mind cannot hold this story of the Son of God who comes to us and makes a home here on earth. It is too fantastical, too mythic.

That the God-Child's brutal death is made even more savage by an ineffable spiritual suffering: the Son of God forced to bear the brute mystery of every creature's deserved karma. And that Christ could lie dead in a tomb, his organs cold and silent, yet somehow, by a power outside of the laws of science, will his own blood to swoosh through his lifeless corpse. It is all a mystery. One I will never explain away. One I hope I will always choose to believe no matter how angrily my intellect fights it. It is all so deeply planted in my knowledge of the world, my longing for rightness and hope and justice, that to not believe would be inconceivable.

Beside me my husband cries, his hands empty and open, his voice off-key, singing the melody toward the empty cross.

PART 4

Terce: Midmorning Prayer

Blessing the work of our hands.
A reminder of the Spirit's nearness.

Let our ears be alert to the stirring call of his voice
crying to us every day: today, if you should hear his
voice, do not harden your hearts.

—The Rule of Saint Benedict

17

Mid-April, Third Week of Easter

In Amarillo, where trees and hills are hard to come by and roads head straight to the edge of the earth, the drama is always in the sky. And no season is more dramatic than spring. West Texans know that the sky always wins when it wrestles land. All year we wait for rain, and when it finally comes it never falls gentle. Rain here is always angry, always flashing the sky and bringing with it wind that drags and tears. No wonder trees hate it here.

After eight years gone, I guess it's odd to say I miss it: The heavy sky and the electric tingle of lightning a mile away. The hairs on my arms lifting toward whatever force draws them from their repose.

I'm home in Texas for the week, visiting my family, sleeping in my childhood bedroom, which is still decorated in bright yellows and pinks with John Keats's words ("More happy love! More happy, happy love!") painted on a mural of hearts. Yes, my seventeen-year-old self was a slightly more earnest, less self-aware version of this thirty-one-year-old. I share a bed in that room with my little boy while Chris travels this week for work. I have no real reason for being here. I'm just here because Chris is away and I've missed my family and the smell of thunderstorms.

This evening August is home with my parents, and I'm in the car with my brother Brooks. We're driving to his friend's house to meet up with his wife Sunny and their small group Bible study. Brooks is telling me about his recent trip to a community that lives in a garbage dump in Nicaragua. He describes the kids he got to know in an orphanage there. He tells me about the boy with special needs he carried on his shoulders for almost five days straight.

I have two older brothers. They're both kind and genuine. They're thinkers. One of my brothers is writer. The other is in full-time ministry. My personality is marked by them in a thousand tiny formulations. Jason taught me to think deeply and work hard. Brooks taught me drama and humor and the fine art of being everybody's favorite.

Brooks was cracking jokes, cutting up in class, and avoiding detentions in the most fantastical ways in high school while I, his three-years-younger sister was overworking, on track to win all the Best Character awards. He was the kind of high school kid who showed up late to his twelfth-grade British lit class by playing dead in the arms of his large actor friend, who burst through the classroom door in the middle of a lecture, wailing, "Don't you die on me! Don't you die on me!" If I remember the story correctly, Brooks and his friend did not get detention; they probably got extra credit for that shenanigan. And that's the story of Brooks's life. Everyone loves him. He's always been the guy who breaks the rules, the guy who convinces everyone else that the rules weren't really that important anyway.

Brooks was married with a kid by the time I graduated college. He was a regular churchgoer. Sometimes he and I would talk theology or make fun of a lame sermon together. But when it came to the deep questions—my calling, my fear that I'd never know what God really wanted of me, my deeper fear that God wasn't really even there—I talked to Jason.

Jason is the one who introduced me to Walt Whitman. He's the one who gave me permission to love poems while the rest of my classmates were making fun of John Donne in high school English. Jason was the artist who painted John Keats's words on my wall, who played guitar and the hammered dulcimer and introduced me to all my favorite singer-songwriters. Jason was the person who passed me the Christian books no one ever mentioned in my Southern Baptist youth group: authors like Brennan Manning and Henri Nouwen. I couldn't believe that my brother read *Catholics,* and his doing so gave me permission to do it as well. When I told him I struggled with doubt, he passed along more books. And those books took me to the mystics and the saints and to a beautiful concept called *mystery.*

Brooks and I cared about each other. We laughed a lot. But we never worked to enter any uncomfortable conversations. It wasn't that I didn't think Brooks had anything to say about the spiritual; it was just that his spiritual life felt layered under a surface I didn't know how to push through. And, honestly, I wasn't brave enough to try.

Eight years into his marketing career, with two kids and a house payment, Brooks experienced a second conversion. In the process of six months, my brother shifted from a hard-surfaced sarcastic churchgoer to a vulnerable seeker. He was clueless about the direction his life was going, but he was listening for the first time. And God was urging him toward full-time ministry. He was becoming the man God had always meant him to be.

That year he quit his job and began a ministry that cares for children and families living in impoverished circumstances. Since then, my brother has become a fixture in some of the most difficult neighborhoods of our hometown. He makes sure the grandma raising the five kids in the apartment in North Grande Villas gets her diabetes medication. He shows up at homes with groceries in hand. He knows when a dad has just been hauled off to prison, and he sits with the kids who've been left behind, again, and lets them cry. He walks down the street, and children come out and run to him. He reads them stories from the Bible and draws pictures with them. My skinny, white brother is fierce on those streets.

While Jason and I veered liturgical in our faith, Brooks has leaned toward the charismatic. He will dance and wave hands and speak words from God to other people. And then he'll crack jokes about all the weird flag waving at his church. Brooks is self-aware enough to know that his charismatic tendencies can make people uncomfortable but brave enough to believe in them anyway. I love that about him. His church has become my charismatic home away from the liturgical. Surprisingly, while I have raised eyebrows at all sorts of charismatic spiritual movements—That girl in college who laughed hysterically when she worshiped God? That lady who claimed her back teeth turned gold because she prayed for it?—I feel loved and cared for by Brooks's church. And most of the time, they don't freak me out.

So when they asked, I agreed to go to small group with Brooks and Sunny. Now I sit in the passenger seat in Brooks's car, watching the clouds gather in the spring evening sky, doing my best to smell the rain before it pours out onto us. I look out the window and pray silently that God will protect me from hearing his voice. *If you want to say something, just say it to me later*, I beg in my head. *I don't like hearing from you at somebody else's small group.*

When people give me messages from Jesus, I'm scared they're right. And I'm scared they're lying. Both have been true in my life before. I'm scared if God talks tonight, it'll be because he's finally coming clean about how much of a disappointment I am.

I arrive with Brooks and smile sweetly, hoping everyone thinks I'm perfectly at ease with my present spiritual state and no one senses that God is making plans to say Something Important. Sunny meets us there and takes me around, introducing me to her friends. When we gather for the study, the group asks me to share about my life right now. I'm not good at hiding my emotions. I tell them it's difficult, lonely. I tell them leaving ministry was harder than I thought it would be. I tell them I'm trying to love San Francisco, but mostly it scares me.

Then I stay quiet. I haven't read the book they're discussing. I listen and twirl the fringe on the throw pillow in my lap. We sit facing one another, some of us on couches, some on dining room chairs that have been spaced throughout the living room. Thirty minutes of discussion passes. Someone prays out loud. And then, just as I think I've made it through in the clear, I hear my name.

A man I hardly know named Jack is looking straight at me and saying in front of the group, "Micha, God wants me to share something with you."

Deep breath.

"Micha, you've spent so many years trying to win God's approval through your own works. That's in the past now," he says.

My heart catches. The hairs on my arms stand. Jack doesn't know. He doesn't know about the years of striving, how my biggest goal as a seventeen-year-old was to win the most awards at my high school, how disappointed I felt the night I was Senior Girl of the Year and nothing had changed. God didn't like me more. There was always more to do, always more ministries to join and Bible studies to lead, more promises to make. When my life really started, then I would please God. When I was done with college, then I would build wells in Kenya and rock sick babies in AIDS orphanages. And then God would be proud of me. There were always more fears to hide and doubts to ignore. There was always less sleep to be had, because surely God would restore my sleep after I did enough for the world.

Jack continues: "San Francisco is full of people who have rebelled against culture, who are longing to see Christ as counter-cultural. Don't be afraid of rebellion."

Don't be afraid of rebellion? *What does that mean?* Then, before I can take another deep breath and ask my insides to calm, Sarah is speaking. Sarah is a girl I grew up with in church. We played together as kids.

"Micha," she says, "I feel like God is showing me a tree in your neighborhood in San Francisco, growing up out of the place where your house is. It was a tree you had to uproot from Philadelphia. And it was a really painful process. But God is saying, 'It's okay to spread your roots now. You can settle, despite the fact that you may not be there long term.'"

She continues: "I have this vision of you and August walking to the park, and the roots following you, making this line in the sidewalk. The tree is following you wherever you go. And as the roots spread out, baby trees are sprouting up from the roots."

I release my breath. How long was I holding it? I'm not sure what to do except to breathe again. What do you do when God talks in human language and you want God to stop talking and you want God to keep talking and you want God to love you and you want God to leave you alone and you want God to prove himself and you want God to stay in the mystery clouds? And there you are in a stranger's living room gripping a throw pillow as if it might protect you from the words of the universe Creator: *That's in the past now*, God says. *The roots are following you*, God says.

You belong where you are, God whispers. *I am following you. I am ahead of you. I am a circle, and you are surrounded.*

They pray for me, this roomful of my brother's friends. Tears gather in my eyes, and I smash them with my thumb before they have the chance to escape. I tremble when I say good-bye. Then I get in the car with my brother. We drive a while under the gray clouds. The sun is setting in pinks and oranges. I think how bold the sky can be, threatening everything and lashing out its beauty. It blinds us and it holds us captive to its plans.

Brooks glances sideways at me as he drives through downtown Amarillo. "Micha," he says, "you're so worried that God is done with you now that you've left the ministry, but God wants you to know it's not over."

I say, "I know you're right." I look out the passenger window so I don't have to look at his face. "I know you're right, Brooks."

But it feels over. It feels like I had a moment in my life to prove my value, to prove my commitment, to make something beautiful, and I couldn't hold the gift I was given. I had these lives to help restore. I had these beautiful high school kids who needed someone to love them, but it was too hard. It was too much time. I was too tired. I began a work I didn't finish.

I feel the words Jack and Sarah and Brooks have said. I hold them between my ribs, moving around in there like a pinball, banging into bones, back and forth and up and down. Brooks and I change the conversation.

When he pulls into our parents' driveway, he throws the car into park and turns to face me. "Micha," he looks in my eyes.

I know. I know, I think.

He wants to say the earnest thing before the moment has passed. Before it's weird again to talk about the spiritual, to speak like God is here with us, zapping the electric current of words between our mouths with cosmic meaning. "God is not done with you," he says, his hands still on the steering wheel.

I open the door and stand on the driveway next to the tree my parents planted when I was born, the tree that was always home base when we played war with the neighborhood kids, the tree that has always dropped its pinecones into the hands of mesmerized preschoolers who receive them like gems. "Thanks," I say, staring hard in his eyes so he knows I mean it.

"You're welcome," he says. "Now, don't go inside and cry all night."

"Who do you think I am?" I laugh. Then I shut the door, and walk the sidewalk toward my parents' house just as the thunder begins its clapping.

❧

August is throwing a tantrum when I step into my parents' living room. It's eight o'clock, and he needs to be in bed. My parents are relieved to see me. August has a stubborn will already, and when it's added to a two-year-old sensibility, it can be brutal. I take over the bedtime routine, and after fifteen minutes of singing and snuggling and reading *Good Night Gorilla*,[1] he finally stops crying. I get him calmed and into bed. My toddler is too small for a big boy bed but too tall for the travel crib at my parents' house. His dad's genes are alive and well in him, making him a year ahead of the norm in his growing. I don't know where he should sleep except in bed with me. So I lay him down and set pillows in the spot where I'll be sleeping later in the night. I sing him to sleep:

> Hey beautiful boy,
> Mama loves you, she loves you.[2]

In the dark, I look around the bedroom I lived in a lifetime ago. I touch August's hair. He's asleep, holding his blanket, "Buppy," his eyelashes thick and heavy on his face.

I tiptoe out of the room, work on the computer for a while, and call my husband to say good night. I want to say something about what happened at the small group, but I don't.

Outside the thunder is still rumbling, and the rain is thick in the night air. My parents' Internet is out, and I'm annoyed. August's bedtime tantrum notched up my inner franticness. *Was that really God tonight? Was it real?* I feel a spark of fire under my skin. Am I angry at God, at the Internet, at my husband? I need to sit and pray and ask God to explain himself. If I don't do it soon, I'll simmer. I'll heat under my skin until the surface melts off and the world is left looking at my raw insides.

How to say this to Chris? Why can't I give it words?

He's happy about his day at work. He's been given a project he's excited about, and he's heading to Atlanta tomorrow morning to meet with several other managers from around the country. I don't know how to break into his happiness with my existential confusion. I want to say to him, "Chris, I think I've been afraid that God is done with me. I've been afraid I ruined my life." But how can I say that on the phone when he's so rarely happy about work? Especially when the life I've chosen, the one I'm afraid God is angry with, is the life I share with him?

The reality is that I hold a constant, gnawing guilt because I never went to live in Nairobi and work at the orphanage school. I hold the unknown faces of children who no one fed, no one rocked, no one read stories to because I never showed up for them. Instead I studied poetry.

And, yes, somewhere during that time of studying poetry, I met my husband. I married him. I never would have met him otherwise. That life of rocking and hugging and reading to the children in Nairobi—the ones I never met—that life is an alternate one. It's not real. It's not true. What is true is that I didn't finish the application form. What is true is that I applied for graduate school, moved to upstate New York, and met my husband three months later. What is true is that I just sang our child to sleep. He would have never existed if I were living in Kenya right now, singing to a room of parentless, sleeping children.

Somehow I am still holding on to both of those realities: That the same God who gave Chris to me is disappointed that I took him and made vows to him and am making a family with him. That the God I claim holds grace out for every failure, every broken choice, is angry for what I left undone across the ocean and in another life I never lived.

I try to pay attention to Chris's words about his flight in the morning and what time he's meeting Mark for lunch.

God's words and Jack's words about what's in the past and Sarah's promise of the roots and all this talk of God not being done with me have stirred up the guilt I've allowed to sit deep under my awareness. How do I begin to say it aloud? Instead I whine about the Internet being out. I tell Chris to have fun in Atlanta. "I'm so happy you get to see Mark and Claire," I say. "Tell them I say hi. Be careful."

I say I love him. I mean it.

I lie down in the bed I'm sharing with my little boy and listen. How many nights have I lain in this bed thinking? When I was in high school and home for college breaks, I used to dream of the sort of woman I would be: brave, willing to sacrifice temporary pleasure for the sake of relieving the hurting. I wanted to be Mother Teresa. I wanted to be Lottie Moon. I wanted to look back at my life as an eighty-year-old and see how the world had more beauty because I lived, because I loved God, because I gave myself wholly to a great calling.

Did I just want to be special? Did I think I needed to earn a Top 10 Percent spot in the holy lineup? Do we ever really have motives that are true and clear?

In bed, I form a prayer in my mind, whispered internally, a line of letters punching words into my skull, letters being read by the Holy Spirit there in Amarillo, Texas, under the clouds. I pray, "You're not done with me?"

I imagine my San Francisco apartment, where the "tree" Sarah spoke of might stand, how beautifully it would unfurl its roots behind me, breaking the sidewalk, pressing through the ground, a fault line pursuing my family and me from front door to playground. I watch little offshoots sprouting trees all over North Beach. I see the homeless man with the black matted hair and the tan trench coat picking fruit from the tree that rises from the ground in our wake.

I hear Jack say, "You've spent so many years trying to win God's approval." I hear Jack say, "That's in the past now."

I close my eyes and listen to the sky until somewhere in the center I quiet, and lean into the dark space.

18

Late April, Fifth Week of Easter

It's a Tuesday when I come to Benedict's words on prayer, when I hear him say how certainty in prayer comes not from "the eloquence and length of all we have to say, but because of the heartfelt repentance and openness of our hearts to the Lord whom we approach."[1] It's April, and it's sunny outside and we've been to the park and had lunch. Now August is napping. The dishes are piled in the sink. I'm two days back from Amarillo, two days back into our daily routine, sitting quiet in the dining room with my afternoon tea. And I laugh when I read the rest of this passage in Saint Benedict's Rule. He says, "Our prayer should, therefore, be free from all other preoccupations and it should normally be short."[2]

I underline. I read it over and over.

"Lord, is this true?" I ask. Have I gotten prayer wrong all this time? All these years of prayer lists and following the proper rules: giving five minutes for God's praise and five minutes for thanksgiving and five minutes for supplication. What if all along, God has just been wishing I would get to the point?

Here, Benedict is talking about corporate prayer. He's talking about monks who pray all day. He's talking about humility and simple faith.

What if all along I've been playing at prayer, performing for a God who didn't want a performance at all? What if all along, all God has wanted was my recognition that I'm needy, that God is necessary? If prayer is mysterious and God doesn't need my "performance," then maybe prayer is less about my words and more about the turning of my heart. Maybe humility doesn't begin until we give up the performance.

I pray in my head: *Jesus, what if this was the point of all those dreams I held for myself? What if this is the point of my fear that I've been failing you all along? So I would realize that what you really long for is not a Micha who is saving the world but a Micha who loves you more than her brave deeds?*

And then I stop praying because Benedict says to keep it short and I'm going to start practicing right now.

19

Early May, Fifth Week of Easter

Chris and I leave August with a friend from church who is making sure he eats his chicken nuggets and gets to bed by eight. We walk out into North Beach, my feet clad in my cutest red-and-white-striped wedges. I hold my husband's hand. We only have to walk two blocks to get to Don Pisto's. Our favorite Mexican restaurant doesn't even have a sign outside its rustic door. It's so cool it doesn't need a sign. We are not so cool. I'm such a visual learner that I can never even remember the name of this restaurant I love.

We give the hostess our name and stand outside in the cool night. Every night here is chilly, but I'm starting to get used to the consistency of the temperature. It's sometimes nice to know you always have to wear a scarf, no matter the season.

"What happened in Amarillo?" Chris asks. August and I have been home for two days, and Chris has been working hard every night, home but stuck in his computer. He knows I've been unsettled. "I had a weird God thing," I said as we were falling asleep my first night back.

"Are you going to tell me about it?" Chris has asked.

"Only if you take me out to dinner first," I whispered, my eyes already closed in the dark.

Now we stand outside the restaurant, our backs pressed against the brick building, the sounds of music and voices filling out and drawing back, an ocean's tide rising and falling from the open door of the restaurant.

"God told me not to be afraid of rebellion," I say, staring straight ahead at the flicker of the glowing pizza sign across the street.

"What does that mean?" His head tilts toward me. He catches my eye and smiles that smile I loved the first night I met him.

"Beats me." I grin back then turn my head from my husband to the street. "You sure you want to know?"

And then I recite the experience aloud to my husband.

You've spent so many years trying to win God's approval.
The roots are following you.
God is not done with you.

By the time we're seated, by the time the sangria is on the table and we're digging chips into guacamole, I've confessed it all to Chris: the fear I'm living with, the same fear I felt when we were dating and I cried hysterically in the movie theater after watching *Nowhere in Africa,* afraid then that I'd already missed my chance to do something important. That was the first time Chris witnessed the depth of my guilt, the shame beneath it.

He's not surprised. We've never been a couple who can hide our inner struggles from each other. Maybe it's grace, a gift that I've never been able to tuck away the thoughts that too often rule my life. My husband knows me. I realize this sitting across the table from him in Don Pisto's. He knows my mind is wild with guilt. Even more, he knows that the guilt is not a lack of love for him or our family. It's not really a fear that he and August are a mistake. It's an irrational shame. I've lived my life ferociously afraid that God had one tight-wound calling for me and I unraveled it, afraid I did irreparable damage that will reverberate out into the cosmos.

I look across the table at this man I loved first because he was kind and funny and knew how to write a sentence and how to tell a joke and how to love a book and how to look in my eyes and say the words that would let me feel known. Here I am again, seven years into our marriage and confessing that I'm afraid *he* was my easy way.

I stare at the freckle on Chris's upper lip and the hard slope of his nose. I love this man. I need him to forgive my second-guessing, hold my confusion for me.

"Micha," Chris pauses and takes a drink. "This God you're talking about? The angry one you'll never please? That's not the God you believe in. You know that, right?"

I nod my head, looking straight at him. My eyes fill with tears. Chris sets his glass on the table. "I want you to stop and listen to yourself for a second. Do you recognize the God you're talking about? He doesn't sound anything like Jesus. You've gotten something desperately wrong, babe."

The waiter shows up with our tacos. I hastily wipe my face as he sets our plates in front of us. When he leaves my husband stares at me, waiting for me to say something.

"I feel crazy, Chris. I feel like I worship and read about and talk about this God who loves me and forgives me and offers grace for my mistakes. And then, secretly, underneath all of that,

I live like grace isn't real, like God is this cruel bully waiting for the perfect chance to show me how much I've messed up his world."

"You know those are different gods, Micha? The good one and the mean one: They're not the same."

I force a tight-lipped smile. "So what you're saying is, you think God is kind and I might be a little loopy?"

He nods his head yes. "I'd never say that." He raises an eyebrow. "Except, yeah. You might be a little loopy, honey."

I grin, tilt my head to the side, and take a huge bite of my taco. Chris laughs but I can see the worry in his face. People who are formed by shame usually hurt the ones who aren't.

20

Mid-May, Sixth Week of Easter

This morning while I pray on the couch Chris calls from our room. "Hey, Mike?" (That's what he calls me when he's in an extra happy mood.) "Can you pick up a chicken for tonight?"

On Monday Chris realized that a few of his coworkers will be heading back to Europe this weekend. These are people who've been living in San Francisco for the past four months, people we've hoped to have over at some point but have never invited. The only night they could make it is tonight, Thursday. So I'm pulling it together. Roasted chicken with lemon and salt and pepper is Chris's classic dinner party dish.

I hear August singing to himself in his room. He's awake and right on time. I set down the Bible I never got around to opening during my fifteen minutes of distracted prayer. August's song will have to be today's benediction. I walk down the hall, open his door and repeat the same poem my mom recited every morning of my childhood:

> Good morning Merry Sunshine!
> How did you wake so soon?
> You scared away the little stars
> And shined away the moon.[1]

My kid is in a great mood. "Mama!" he shouts and holds up his fleece-covered arms. I lift him out of his crib and whisper, "I need the biggest hug ever!" August squeezes with all his might. In our small apartment, it's only about four long hops from his room to ours. So I literally hop. One, two, three, four! I pretend to throw him onto the bed where Chris is reading the news on his phone, then gently drop him into the soft covers and pillows. He crawls up his dad's body and snuggles while simultaneously poking Chris's face. I leave to get some food ready. A couple of minutes later, Chris brings August into the dining room, and I present breakfast: plain yogurt, honey, and granola.

"A-mee!" August shouts as I fasten the rubber bib around his neck.

Translation? *Amen.* My son's newfound holiness is hilarious to me. He said this before lunch yesterday, and I had forgotten to tell Chris. All I can figure is that after a short lifetime of hearing prayers before meals, my son has assumed that "Amen" should be exclaimed before consuming any food.

I move to pour myself some cereal, and when I bring it in to the table, I notice Chris still standing in the dining room in his boxers, hands on his hips, gazing out the window with a stern jaw like some undressed superhero. Obviously, he's thinking about something very important.

"We should have roasted potatoes with rosemary and lots of butter," he says, eyes fixed on the unimpressive tree branch in front of the alley.

There is my husband, stuck in his happy food place, thinking of this dinner party, no doubt already having moved on to the place settings and the possibility of a signature cocktail.

"Yes, we should," I say.

He looks at me, confused. "Have potatoes?" I say.

"Yeah, yeah," he says. "Will you pick them up? The little fingerling ones."

I set my bowl on the table and move to him, raise my hands to his shoulders like we're in eighth grade and Bryan Adams is crooning from the speakers.

"I'm really excited for you to meet Daniel and Brigitte," he says. And then you know the rest of the team, right?"

"I think so."

Chris leads a group of salespeople at his job. This dinner party is going to somehow provide enough food to serve all eight of them and me. There's absolutely no room in our house for a ten-person dinner party. Thankfully, Chris and I like a social challenge. We may both be terrible at details and incapable of returning library books on time, but we thrive at feeding people and forcing them into our tiny dining room.

Chris still has super hero face.

"And brussels sprouts? And salad?" I ask.

He looks at me, nods his head.

"And if you think of anything else. Just tell me. I'm going to the store this afternoon."

"Yeah . . ." He's still window gazing.

"Buddy."

"Hm?"

"It's seven fifteen, and you're cutting it close." He doesn't move. "Good grief. Get out of this room!" I slap his boxer-clad butt and send him in the direction of the shower.

࿓

When I was in youth ministry, Chris and I both loved the motion of our home. High school kids watched movies on our living room floor or came by after school just to talk and play with the baby. College-aged volunteer leaders dropped by for dinner and sometimes slept on the couch. I miss the feeling of offering someone else a safe place. I miss making tea and sitting down for long chats. I miss hospitality.

I've never been much of a decorator or cook. I don't flit around the kitchen playing with food like some artist. Cooking is stressful and demanding for me. And I feel absolutely no therapeutic release in the scrubbing of dishes. None. What I love is people. I want to ask them questions, refill their drinks, listen to their stories, make space for them in my home.

The problem with loving only the human connection aspect of hospitality is that somebody still needs to clean the house and cook the food or the people don't show up at my door. A girl has got to sweep the floor before company arrives. People need to eat, and dinner is the best way to get somebody to sit down and talk.

Chris and I are a good team. He plans the meals, picks out the wine. He hums while he makes dinner, and I hum while I set the table. But all those hours before the setting of the table, I am not humming. I am anxious. I'm not anxious about cleaning the house or shopping for groceries. I am anxious because doing those things makes me feel like a "housewife." The difference is subtle, and it's mostly in my head. In my former working days, if I frantically cleaned my house after a long day of work, rushing to get the bathroom shined before company arrived, I felt I'd *earned* my stress. Working women have a right to sigh and huff.

But today, as I spend August's nap time not writing or reading but ironing a tablecloth and napkins, vacuuming, and scrubbing the toilet, I recognize a lie slithering up into my brain: *This is all you do with your life*, it says. *Your husband works all day while you iron napkins in an adorable floral apron. You are nothing more than a housewife.*

I mop the floors, and I imagine what Chris's female coworkers probably think of me and my life. I picture them snickering behind my back about my ironing in the middle of the afternoon while they were closing deals and walking down granite hallways in pointy-toed shoes.

Then, in the middle of that thought, I stop mopping. I prop the mop against the wall and look at my apron, which is absolutely as adorable as the lie in my brain said it was. Then I turn to stare at the ironed tablecloth and the half-mopped floor. I sit down on the hardwood beside the bucket and force myself to say it out loud.

"Lord," I say, "I am not ironing and mopping because I have nothing better to do. I am ironing and mopping because I get to take care of some people who deserve to be taken care of."

I sit there with my eyes closed, and I feel God's nearness, the weight of the Spirit pressing in. I imagine God laying his hands on my head and pulling out the lie. His fingers pinch the gray cloud of a thought then he throws it out. "Thank you," I whisper. And God leaves his hands on my head a moment longer.

I stand up and grab the mop, thinking of Benedict's words: *Prayer should normally be short.* "I am not a failure. I'm not a failure, because you love me," I pray, and I finish the floors.

I pour drinks and ask questions and sit beside our guests and listen to all the work stories. We eat the dinner my husband cooked and wipe our mouths with the cloth napkins I folded. Then I watch the crowd leave my home for a walk around the neighborhood. They're off with Chris to find gelato and grab a drink at his favorite bar. Brigitte and Daniel hug me, and I stand at the front door to wave them away. Of course I can't join them. August is asleep in his room. This is Chris's last chance to spend time with these friends before they move.

I have a creeping resentment, though. Once again, I am the one stuck at home, the one left with the dishes. But as I stand at the open door, watching their mass exodus into the lights of Grant Street, I remember: Today is a miracle day. It's a day when God is pressing in, separating lies and truths. I think, *I get to practice hospitality right now. I get to be very Benedictine.*

Saint Benedict mentions "hurrying" twice in his rule. The monks are to hurry to the work of God, and they are to hurry to welcome the stranger.[2] They're not hurrying to their physical labor. They aren't hurrying to meet a deadline. They're not even hurrying toward good deeds. They are urgent about two things only: prayer and hospitality.

I've spent so much of my life in a hurry, snapping at my son to get his shoes on, hastily buckling him in his car seat even though he wants to do it himself. *We don't have time*. But am I urgent about the things that matter?

What am I rushing toward? Politeness? Do I hurry so that people will think I'm good enough, worthy enough? *Make haste*, Benedict says. *Make haste toward the stranger*. Notice the unnoticeable.

I lean my head against the doorframe and close my eyes as our guests' voices grow muffled in the night-distance. I breathe a prayer that I would choose this moment, right here, to rush toward love.

Then I walk straight to the kitchen. Without feeling shame for my failures as a liberated woman, I carry each dish to the sink. I wash. I rinse. I sing songs. And I believe, maybe for one of the first times, that out of that group of nine people I shared a meal with, I am the one being blessed.

PART 5

Sext: Midday Prayer

The hour of light.

Vision.

Healing.

God comes to us disguised as our life.

—Paula D'Arcy

21

Late May, First Week of Ordinary Time

I want to have a second baby.

I've been playing this in my mind for a couple of months. While some friends were set on getting pregnant as soon as their little ones were walking, I hesitated. I've always seen myself as having more than one kid, but the idea of pregnancy and morning sickness and those long last weeks before giving birth, and then, of course, birth itself, tends to leave me more anxious than inspired. For the past year, I've been aware of the small fire burning in my belly for another child, but I've been doing my best to douse it. It's not because I don't like being a mom. It's the idea of pregnancy—the fear of it—that rises above any longings I have for a houseful of kids.

Maybe I have a very low pain tolerance. That's another way of saying I'm a wuss. I vomited almost every day of pregnancy from six weeks until fifteen weeks with August. And though I trained myself for a natural delivery, hypnobirthing and a birth center and a midwife, few of my plans lined up when it came to getting August out of my body. I wanted it to be peaceful and beautiful. My memories of those twenty-two hours of labor are fearful and sharp and torched with fluorescent light.

But the past couple of months, I've felt it simmering to the surface, this longing for a baby in my arms again. Two weeks ago, August stood before me on the bathroom stool, a toothbrush dangling from his mouth, nude except for the rain boots he insisted on wearing after bath time. I listened to his long babbling story of a rocket and a shark, toothpaste creeping from the corners of his mouth. I washed his face and rinsed his toothbrush while he kept on talking, and I stared in awe at the little boy on the stool recounting a tale I hardly understood. My baby wasn't there; August was a kid.

I've been wondering what gives us courage, what makes a desire grow fat enough with hope that it miraculously weighs heavier, larger than our fears. *How can I go through pregnancy again?* becomes, *How could I not?* Out of nowhere, in the middle of this transition and sadness and loneliness, I feel brave.

I want August to have a sibling to share his life with. I look at our little family at the dinner table and sense an empty seat. There are more of us to come.

Chris and I started talking about it in January, wondering if we might be ready for another baby. Should we even be feeling drawn to another child, when Chris's work is unhappy and my sanity is a bit unfettered? Is pregnancy an excuse to take our minds off our current confusion?

But what if that's not what it is at all? What if the possibility of another child is a bright-lit room we should walk boldly into? We both began to pray about it on our own. That empty space inside me has been a secret idea I've held up in my quietest moments. How often have I asked this question: *How do you know when God says yes?*

Maybe God's yes is sometimes his hand stroking the anxious bird that pecks away in the mind. I have a lot of birds pecking in my brain, flapping their wings, and building nests anywhere they can find a cozy spot. Lately, though, I've been thinking that God's hands know how to touch and calm their frantic nesting, offer them a way out of my mind: a window to perch then soar out of.

Last month, that bird—the one pecking over pregnancy and baby—stopped flapping. It quieted its restless chirping and, one day (*swoosh!*) flew right out of its window perch.

It wasn't some lightning bolt of peace. It wasn't that either Chris or I finally knew this was the certain future for our family. It's just that Chris was standing in the kitchen making a cream sauce for the pasta and I thought, *How can I not have another baby with this man?"* And I told him so.

He looked back over his shoulder at me and said in his sexiest voice, "That's what they all say."

And that was that.

22

Mid-June, Fourth Week of Ordinary Time

We stand at the bar in Absinthe, sipping cocktails. It's our sixth anniversary. I wear a gray silky dress cut so low that when I saw myself in the mirror at home, my inner good girl demanded I safety-pin the neckline a bit higher. I wear black heels and my darkest lipstick.

August is in bed by now; the babysitter is probably studying at the dining room table. Chris and I stand watching a plethora of San Franciscans come through this restaurant.

I love this city for its wild collection of people in such a small space. San Francisco is roughly seven miles wide and seven miles long, an area encompassing some of the greatest tech minds on earth, thriving immigrant communities, the world's most vibrant gay community, artists, writers, and hippies. Sometimes I look at my husband and say, "Tell me again how we got here?"

Chris isn't sure either.

We watch a musician prop up a cello in its case and lean against the bar. I listen to her conversation with her friend. They're on their way home from their performance at the symphony two blocks from here. They discuss the piece of music they just played. As I eavesdrop, I turn to catch my husband's eye. "You know I have to listen," I whisper. "There's lots of drama because they were playing Bach tonight, and this other cellist can't get his part right so they're super annoyed." I smile wide.

The room begins to fill with symphony-goers crowding around the bar just as Chris and I finally take our seats at a table. We graze on cheese and olives, holding hands and reviewing the past six years. "Remember those summer nights in Devon when we ate cheese and olives on the porch at least twice a week?" Chris says, popping an olive into his mouth.

"Yeah, because we couldn't plan a meal in advance. Ever." I spread cheese on a slice of bread. "We waited till we got home from work every night and then sat around moaning about what to eat for dinner for, like, two hours. Then we finally ate cheese."

"But it was really good cheese. That aged gouda?"

"And prosciutto and kalamata olives."

"Remember how it felt like we'd never figure our lives out?"

"Not much has changed," I say.

He laughs and looks up to motion for the waiter. "We were happy, though. When you weren't weeping inconsolably." He raises his eyebrows and grins.

"Yep. Like I said: Not much has changed."

Chris grabs my hand across the table, and I smile, thinking how his existence, the very grace that such a man would walk into my life and accept me in all my complexity, is a daily reminder that God exists and loves me.

At the same time, five blocks away, a couple of guys decide our car is worth exploring. They shatter our window, reach in for the outrageously old GPS, and sprint away when someone screams.

Chris finds the car just a few minutes after the police. I stand in the humming restaurant waiting for a ride that never comes and eventually find myself on the sidewalk beside my husband and the police, my darling heels cracking shattered glass.

We drive home with the broken window taped over. We park on a neighborhood street and walk to our apartment hand in hand. Before we go to bed, Chris tells me he received an e-mail from our landlord during dinner. He didn't want to ruin the night. But, since it had already been shattered (literally), he fills me in on the e-mail's contents. Our landlord has decided to break our lease, kick us out of the apartment, and sell it. Happy anniversary to us.

৵৵

I sweep the floors this morning while August follows me around the house with his pretend vacuum, sometimes "helping" and sometimes screaming for me to stop. Chris is outside with the car, meeting with the insurance company about the damage done during the Great Anniversary Break-In. Amazingly, though our window was wrecked, nothing was stolen from our car except for that five-year-old GPS. All morning I've been mouthing *Thank you* to Jesus for the Good Samaritan who screamed at the hoodlums while they ransacked my car.

I could not care less about that old GPS. What wears me out is the detail-management in the aftermath: taking the car to the shop, installing a new window. I'd rather have my stuff stolen than be forced to fill out paperwork about it. I could not be more grateful that Chris is the one outside right now.

I move the broom across the wooden hallway, angling it deep into the corners where the dust bunnies gather, my mind heavy with the loss of this apartment: *Do we really have to move again, eight months in? Can our landlord really break the lease and force us out?* The burden of leaving our home with its sweet closet-sized toddler bedroom and skinny kitchen is too much today. I take the vacuum to the rug in the living room and let it do all the roaring for me.

Is this stability? I wonder under the noise of the vacuum. Is stability the vow you live out in the insignificant details of ordinary life? The vacuuming? Building the wooden tower so your kid can knock it down? Is it washing the dishes and putting them away, even though tonight someone will slap pasta all over that dinner plate again?

I'm surprised that the thought of leaving our apartment has led me back again to Saint Benedict and his vows. I look over at August, who rolls his pretend vacuum right next to mine. "Watch me, Mama! Watch me!" he screams at the top of his lungs over the thundering. He moves it back and forth and growls.

I know this: Stability isn't this apartment. It isn't even this city or any other city I haven't remained in. And stability isn't my old life on the East Coast or my old life in Texas. *Stability is not something you do.* This thought comes from heaven, like manna. It sits on my tongue, and I taste it.

Stability isn't a test I already failed. I look at August playing beside me. He runs his vacuum into mine, and I say, "Oh no! Crash!" He laughs and does it again.

I haven't ruined this. God is the giver of faithfulness and consistency. God is stable. I've spent a lot of these past nine months feeling guilty for leaving Chris's family. And before that, I held guilt for leaving my own. I've spent so much of my life hoping to prove that I'm still a good daughter despite my missing family pizza night every Friday. That I'm still a good friend despite the e-mails I can't find time to return, the phone calls I don't make but obsess over. That I'm still a good mother even though I lose my temper and scream at this little person I love most in the world.

I try but have never made myself good enough. I always come up lacking.

I move the coffee table and run the vacuum over those ghost circles where the table legs stand. August *vrooms* his vacuum into mine again. I yell, "Smash!" and "Boom!" and "Owie!" He laughs.

I think about that revival preacher who said we could live a day without sin, and I remember that longing for someone to stand up and counter him, for someone to promise me that sinlessness wasn't the ultimate hope of faith.

I was desperate then, and I'm desperate now. I wanted something matching Paul's words in the book of Ephesians, his prayer that the followers of Jesus might have power to "grasp how wide and long and high and deep is the love of Christ."[1] I think of that sort of filling as if God's love were a balloon growing inside me, changing shape so it expands into my limbs and my head. *Wholeness*, I think. *Stability doesn't lead to perfection. It leads to wholeness.*

Jesus fills me, and that is how I learn stability. Joan Chittister says stability is found in the everyday. There will always come "a day when this job, this home, this town, this family seem irritating and deficient beyond the bearable," she says. The spiritual work of stability happens then. When the lover is no longer the keeper of a young, beautiful body. When the children quit their sweetness. When the house is falling apart or *being taken away*. When the window is shattered and someone has to clean the mess up.

"Stability enables me to outlast the dark, cold places of life until the thaw comes and I can see new life in this uninhabitable place again. But for this to happen, I must learn to wait through the winters."[2]

My whole life I have sung songs and read verses and even taught high school students the passages about Jesus washing us whiter than snow, cleansing the deep, mysterious caverns within our hearts. But I have never understood what it could mean for Jesus to wash the panic from my mind.

I have known God since I was a little girl. I have met with God on swing sets and beside rivers and in the faces of the children I met at orphanages in Nairobi. I believe God offers a much bigger life than one in which we obsess over our moral imperfections. But, somehow, my psyche brings me back to my failures. Over and over I meet God and find the Holy Spirit holding open doors to a three-dimensional world. But most of the time I'm content with flat vision.

I look down at August. "Ahhh!" he yells as we finish the corners of the rug. I flip the switch off, and the world quiets. He turns to me and smiles. No, stability is not about this house, this city. It's much bigger than *my* choices to remain or leave. To pursue stability, I must first believe that God is stable, that God is offering me a whole world right here in my ordinary existence. Here in the "raw material of the average daily life," as Chittister says. The life Benedict lays out is a simple one, she says. "It asks for no great physical denials and gives no great mystical guarantees."[3]

The sort of worship Benedict was asking of his monks is far from the sort I find in my spirit most of the time. Too often I'm replaying my shame on repeating cassettes in an unsettled mind, reminding myself of who and why I've failed. Benedict says to simplify. He says to do the physical work in front of me, to do it unto God. Not from guilt, not from fear, but as an offering that God might take it and make it beautiful.

I unplug the cord and wrap it around and around the back of the vacuum. Then I drag it down the long hallway, wheeling along the wooden floor.

"Come pay wid me! Come pay!" August yells from his room, where he holds five puzzle pieces, dropping them as he walks to the living room. I gather the rest from his closet and pick up the lost pieces strewn through the hallway. We sit on the fresh-swept rug in the living room, working slow to make a Very Hungry Caterpillar.

Chris comes back from taking care of the car and closes the door behind him. "Okay, I'm taking the car to the shop at three o'clock," he says and steps into the hallway onto a Cheerio that August must have dropped in the past two minutes. I hear it crunch.

"Ugh," I moan. "I just vacuumed."

"Sorry, babe." he says and leaves the crumb pile and his shoes by the front door. He walks into the living room, and I make a sad face to mirror his.

"Is it all that bad?" I ask, searching his eyes.

My husband falls onto the couch and sighs. He looks around at our home.

"Nah," he smiles with his lips pressed tight. "I mean, the car will be fine. The GPS barely worked, and I didn't even like this apartment anyway."

"Yes, you did," I say. "You're such a lying liar. You love this place."

"Yep," he says and reaches for his computer. "Which is why I'm gonna research tenant laws right now. Who knows if a landlord can even kick us out? We signed a year lease."

"This is turning out to be your dream Saturday. Car insurance conversations and tenant laws! You want to eat lunch? Or would you rather be hungry all afternoon just to make it more dramatic?"

"Oh, I'll eat," he says. "But first: suffering." He opens his laptop.

I sit cross-legged on the rug and look at our son. He's babbling about the caterpillar's fruit in the picture. "Here's the strawberry!" I say, holding out a piece of the puzzle. "Do you see any other pieces that are red like a strawberry?" And my little boy's hands dig around the pile until he holds up a piece, smiling.

"Dis!" he says. "Dis one is twabearwy"

And it fits together. Just like that we fasten those pieces on the floor into a picture, into something impermanent, something whole.

23

Late June, Fifth Week of Ordinary Time

I've been in therapy before. I spent several months of our second year of marriage figuring out why I was so sad. I've been much more competent with my own mind since those hourlong sessions with the counselor in an empty church classroom in Newtown Square, Pennsylvania.

But here I am, five years later, feeling the darkness slink back in again. Finally I'm recognizing it, this black smoke settling into the creases of my mind. I don't think I'm depressed, but

I do think something's wrong; something has been wrong for several months. All this time I've written it off as loneliness, homesickness. But I know there's more. I know it has to do with prayer.

I've decided to start seeing a spiritual director. I want a new canvas, a fresh way to make sense of all I believe about God but can't seem to practice in my prayer life. I keep going back to my husband's words: that I secretly believe in two different gods, the kind one and the mean one. No wonder I can't connect prayer with God's mercy and healing.

It's Tuesday, and August and I are off to his new one-room preschool, a five-minute walk from our apartment. The school is a toddler-aged program that combines play and art a couple of mornings a week. On his first day I took an official "first day of school ever" photo of August on our porch, standing proud with his gray fleece zipped up snug and chest puffed out. He was terrified when we got there, but eventually he had fun, and I only cried outside the door for five minutes, which I considered a great success. His second day he was brave, and there were no tears. Today is the third.

I walk with him down the sidewalks, jumping cracks and holding hands. We walk past the old people in the park practicing Tai Chi and past the huge Catholic cathedral where morning mass is ending and souls are scurrying out of the building and off to their working lives. We wait at Columbus Avenue for the light to flash green, and when it does I hold August's hand with my ninja-mama-grip, the kind that somehow clamps his hand and wrist at the same time, assuring that if he tries to let go and run away from me, I will pull his arm off before I let him loose.

When we make it to the school, the bottom flat of a typical

San Francisco house, he walks right in like he belongs there. He crouches down where another little boy is setting up train tracks with one of the teachers and immediately gets to work. I stick his Thomas the Tank Engine backpack into his cubby and lean over to give him a kiss. He hardly notices as I walk out the door.

There's such a strange tension in handing your child over to people you don't know, even people with certifications and kind demeanors in a sweet room decorated with wall-sized, kid-painted papier-mâché flowers. How odd is it that we place our most precious possessions in the hands of near-strangers and then walk away? And isn't it even more odd that we do it in order to stay sane? Prior to my grandparents, my ancestors never tried to raise children all on their own. They lived in communities where in-laws and parents were down the road or across the field. Sisters and lifelong friends were a part of their every day. The responsibility for child-rearing was held by everyone in a community. Now parents like me exist, trying to raise our kids with family thousands of miles away, doing as much research as we can in hopes that we will choose caregivers who will love our children and do right by them. But who can really know?

Guilt is like a tide pool at the base of my insides. It's always there, though sometimes I hardly notice it. And then, without warning, the tide flows in and the pool overflows. I feel it rise inside all the way to my neck. I keep walking away from the school, engorged by that tidal pool, certain that my body was never meant to hold this, certain my skin will burst and all that will be left of me is a sopping mess on the concrete. *I chose to live across the continent from all the people who love my boy*, I think. And then I breathe slow and stop at the corner of Mason and Chestnut for a cappuccino. The barista shapes the foam into two pretty leaves, and I drink it carefully because it's beautiful.

I walk the few blocks to the car then drive to my spiritual director's office. This is our second meeting. I spent the first weeping about how August is waking up too early and I'm not getting up early enough and I don't know how to pray anymore. I had convinced myself I was going to a spiritual director in hopes of learning some new tools for prayer. What I didn't realize was how fragile I am, how Debby's few questions about what prayer looks like for me would lift something dark from its hidden inner place. I heard myself trying to prove to her that I do love Jesus. Really, I think I was just trying to prove it to myself.

This morning Debby stands beside her desk in sneakers, running pants, and a zip-up jacket. Her blonde and gray-streaked hair has been pulled back into a hasty ponytail. When I walk in, she smiles and apologizes for her clothes. "I'm going for a run as soon as we're through here."

She sits down in a worn, stuffed chair facing a floral-patterned love seat that I swear must have been lifted straight from my Easter dress in 1993. There's something calming about taking that seat among the rose and cream flowers.

Last time I sat down in her office, I felt an inner panic that she'd ask me to pray out loud. It's not that praying out loud is hard for me or that I'm intimidated. It's more that I'm pretty good at it, at least if we're talking about my use of pauses and rhythm, my ability to say something meaningful or moving. Sometimes I pray aloud, and the outward expression matches the inner truth. But too often, I'm the actress and prayer is my stage. I'm too aware of myself, too aware of everyone else's response.

Debby begins our session by asking me to pray silently as she leads. We sit in silence for a minute or two, and then she speaks to me in our quiet. My eyes are squeezed shut, and I work to shrug loose the heavy burden of coming to God from my back. I want some sort of release.

"Micha," she says, "I want you to ask God to give you a word or phrase to focus on. I want you to ask God what he wants you to hear today, what he wants you to take with you."

We're quiet for a moment. She speaks again, "Micha, don't put pressure on this. Just ask for it as a gift, no demands."

I begin to form the request in my mind, speaking silently to the Holy Spirit, *Will you give me a word or a phrase?* I ask. And then, as quickly as the question is formed, I think, *Whatever phrase comes to my mind will probably just be me convincing myself that God is speaking.* I shake that thought, try to focus.

Then I think, *What if God doesn't give me a word at all? Will I just make one up?*

My mind is such an annoying roommate. *Settle down,* I command it. Then I pray again that I might believe with honesty and fullness of heart. I say to myself, *No, I will not make up a word. I won't pretend. I'll be honest with Debby.*

I try again. *God, my head wants me to think that I'm just deceiving myself into believing that any word might come from you. Please show me it's possible. Please be here and give me a word that isn't my own.*

And then, like that, despite myself, I watch a word rise from the bottom of a dark pool, small at first and then larger and brighter. It rises into my vision. *Believe,* it says. *Believe.*

Debby is still there. "Micha, look at that word God has given you. Look at your life, every part of it." She lets her words sit in the air for a while. My elbows are still on my knees. I lean forward, letting my head droop toward the ground, my eyes closed to the room and the floral couch. "What does that word mean for how you see your time at home with August, how you see yourself? What does that word say to how you see yourself in your marriage, in your calling, in your struggle with life after ministry, in your friendships?"

I watch as each part of my life floats up to my awareness. What does it mean to believe God is good in the midst of the ordinary moments at home with August when I'm most happy, most fulfilled but also when I'm most bored, most vulnerable? Can I believe my value is greater than my career title in those afternoons when I look at my hands folding towels and think, *Is this really what I do with my life?* What does it mean to believe I am utterly loved when I am so frustrated that three days have passed and I still have not worked on the book I long to write? What does it mean to *believe*? In my marriage? In my attempts at meaningful friendships? Can I believe in God's nearness? Can I believe in God's goodness in every ordinary moment of my life?

We sit in silence awhile, and she asks me to open my eyes. "What did God say to you? What word did God give you?" she asks.

"Well, first I spent several minutes trying to convince myself that God might actually speak to me. That took a long time." I look up at her and grin.

"Did God speak to you?"

"I think so." I look down at my hands, where I'm mindlessly spinning my wedding ring around my left ring finger. "I asked God to speak to me anyway, even though I probably wouldn't believe it was him."

Debby smiles. "What did God say?"

"He said, *Believe.*"

Debby is quiet for a moment, looking at me. "What do you think that means, Micha?"

I gaze past Debby's head at the bookshelves. Then I look back down to my hands. What does it mean to believe? Isn't that the question every theologian has ever set out to understand?

"Well, maybe it means I have the chance to notice how Jesus is making my ordinary life into something beautiful." My voice catches. Am I crying? I take a deep breath. "I think it means that belief happens in all of my life, not just in the moments I choose to pray or not to pray." I grab a tissue from the box beside me. I keep surprising myself lately. How have I not known how hurt I've been by my own prayerlessness? How lonely I've been for God's voice?

Yet somehow, while I speak to Debby, while I weep for this word and all it whispers to my life, I feel detached from it all, as if I've risen above myself and am watching my own tears. How can I love God so much that his speaking this word is the best news I've heard all day? And how, at the same time, can I peer down on my body sitting on the floral couch and think, *Am I deluding myself?*

But even as I speak this word out loud—*Believe*—I hold hope. God might be asking of me the hardest and the most beautiful thing, and God might be asking it in love.

"I think it means God wants to make my mind into something healthy, even though it's entangled in a lot of doubt and guilt," I say. And that word *entangled* suddenly makes so much sense.

We sit in silence. I imagine God's hands combing through that matted mess, the way my mother once worked through my hair that day I'd let my friend play beauty shop with me in third grade. Carey had tied knot after knot until a ball of torn and fuzzy hairs sat on my head. When my mother came to the rescue, she moved slowly around my scalp. She sprayed and picked and released hair after hair from the knot. Her work bored and hurt me. A few times she must have thought she would have to cut that mass of hairs to free my scalp of its burden. But still, she worked.

Maybe belief is patience. Maybe it's letting God untangle every small knot. Maybe freedom comes gently.

Debby looks at me, and I wipe the corners of my eyes with the tissue in my hand. She says, "Believe. What an invitation."

"Yes," I say. I lean back against the couch and sigh. An invitation.

24

Late June, Fifth Week of Ordinary Time

I stand at the crib of my almost-two-year-old and sing songs I want to pass down, hymns I learned in the dim-lit sanctuary of my childhood where every worship service, even the Sunday night once-a-year youth musical, ended with an altar call, an invitation for any soul longing for reconciliation with God to come boldly to the altar and be transformed.

"What if the one night we didn't have an invitation was the night some soul missed his chance at Jesus?" I once heard a country preacher say. That thought, that the Holy Spirit needed minor-keyed hymns and anxious pew-standers wandering their eyes throughout the room for that one lost person to make a choice to follow Jesus, was an idea that ran through the veins of my church culture.

The invitation hymns are the richest of the Baptist musical

canon. They're the most earnest, the most demanding, and sometimes, amazingly, the gentlest. My childhood faith is a complicated thing, full of fear and beauty, life and guilt. But of all that was planted into my soul's early soil, the kindest truths came from the old hymns.

> *I have decided to follow Jesus*
> *No turning back, no turning back.*[1]

> *All to Jesus, I surrender. All to him I freely give. . . .*
> *I surrender all, I surrender all.*[2]

> *Just as I am without one plea . . .*
> *Oh Lamb of God, I come, I come.*[3]

Those songs are burned into my heart's flesh. They were my earliest notions of spiritual surrender. We'd sing the hymns and watch for God to do something, anything. Usually someone would come forward, sometimes a man struggling with alcoholism and hoping to piece his life back together, or a teenager certain God was calling him to be a pastor. But usually people came to get saved. Often they were children like me, raised in the church. We all knew that eventually we'd have to "decide to follow Jesus." It was always our choice.

Choices are a terrible and wonderful thing.

Even as a seven-year-old, I grasped the power of the kind but heavy hand of God that asked for a yielding of my control even as it held out the sweet relief of Jesus' love. I was entranced by the notion that God wanted me, just as I was. I'd sing the hymns and sway behind the polished wooden pew.

The night I made my first and most significant vow to follow Jesus, I walked down the long aisle, not out of fear, but with the courage of serious faith. Never had I felt so hot and fluttery inside. Never had I known God to come so boldly near. I felt a Spirit wind breathe me out of my place in the pew, push against my legs as they carried me, alone, toward the front of the sanctuary. My heart obeyed my feet. I found myself, a second grader, standing before my congregation, waiting for some adult to show up and tell me what I was doing there.

Thirty minutes later, I had prayed for Jesus to forgive my sins. I'd given God my heart, that abstract and certain center of me. Two weeks later, I was baptized. I still recognize the Holy Spirit by the heavy inner heat in my chest. I may hesitate to believe, but I know the *otherness* I felt that night.

The invitation hymns demand the question, *What is God asking me to do?* I ask that question in fear and amazement but almost always with a tight-clenched space in my belly where anxiety crouches beside the melodies.

When I was a kid, we sang country hymns at MeeMaw and PawPaw's house some Sundays after lunch. MeeMaw would sit at the piano and Aunt Cissy would pull out her cello, Dad his violin. ("Fiddle," MeeMaw called it.) Cissy's husband, Ed, would grab his "gee-tar," and if Aunt Rita was in town, it was a real party. She's a flautist. PawPaw could play anything, but his greatest instrument was his voice, a deep bass, and his inherent knowledge of all the bass lines. MeeMaw's vibrato would quiver, and the rest of us would join in, my brothers rolling their eyes and making faces at me across the dining room, where the table had been cleared. We sat together singing, "I'll Fly Away" and "Great Day in the Morning."

Hymns gathered us. They were our culture, our history, our connection to one another and to our ancestors. We were never from a *place* the way some Americans say they're Italian or German. We came from sharecroppers, the poor of the South, who eventually made their way to cheaper land on the plains of Texas. Our people had lost their vaguely European heritage generations back. We had faith. And music.

Somehow I knew, when I felt the *whoosh* of the wind and the bright burn of the sun, or watched the stars punch through the black night with my dad, who always knew every constellation, that the hymns and the sky and the safety of my family were connected. *Just as I am*, there in my driveway at eight o'clock on a school night, holding my daddy's hand and staring with him at the magic of the sky.

Somehow in this great big universe, I was safe, hemmed in by loving parents. And somehow I was in terrifying danger: That God might not forgive me. That hell might be my destiny no matter how many times I'd lain in bed in the darkness and asked Jesus into my life. Even though the preachers promised "once saved, always saved," it still felt improbable to believe my child-sized commitment to Jesus would ever hold tight enough.

My early fear of God is a complicated thing. Most of my memories in the church sanctuary are beautiful: lit with an orange glow, my mother's simple and sweet alto drifting down to my place beside her. In my memories I am at home in that space, standing on the cushioned golden seat of the pew with my left arm around my dad, staring with him into our shared hymnal. I belonged to a loving community, one that knew me and welcomed me.

To say I was loved there must ring confusing to anyone who wants to understand the source of my fear. How can a loving church be unsafe? In my memories, church turned dangerous when strangers entered and took over: the revivals twice a year and the obligation of showing up each weeknight for a series of evangelistic sermons. The traveling preachers who blew through our sanctuary always made a mess of the sweet home I lived in.

Saint Benedict wrote about stability for a reason: committed community leads to humility and humility leads to wisdom. A life of skipping from church to church and being hailed as a gifted "man of God" usually creates a heightened sense of one's own power. Power without community makes for carelessness. The culture of evangelistic revivals was often meanness disguised as eternal concern.

I don't remember the faces or names of the men who preached the revivals in my childhood church, but their words seared my heart in ways that have never been undone. Every time some evangelist asked for "every head bowed and every eye closed," every time I was asked to raise my hand if I wasn't "absolutely certain, beyond a shadow of a doubt" that if I died on my way home from the church—my eight-year-old body in the hands of my father who just might drive our gray '84 Caravan head-on into the coming headlights—I would "be in heaven that very night," my stomach ached in fear, and I wondered if that feeling was God telling me I'd gotten it wrong. I hadn't believed *enough*.

Some children wade lightly in the words they hear in sermons. The river water runs past their feet and wets them. Some, like me, tiptoe into the water only to be flooded beneath its current. They eventually come to the surface, but they never stop gasping for air. I listened to the men preach my probable death, my unintentional eternity in hell, and their god was formed in me. His image was menacing and threatening.

That god demanded I try again and try again and get it right this time, a perfectionist piano teacher who wished my fingers were better shaped for the keys. My petition, my longing for his mercy, my longing to do right by him: these were the roots of my future chaotic faith. I struggle to see that any words those preachers spoke came from Jesus at all because what I remember is so far off course from the other God I knew, the God my parents preached with their simple lives, the God who loves me in the Gospels. I'm still unweaving that tight braid: the angry god pleated and wound around the God of love.

With every head bowed and every eye closed, I didn't pray for salvation those nights of early doubt. Instead, I begged God to let us make it home without the foretold car crash. And after we pulled into the driveway, safe, I climbed into my bed, clenched the covers tight across my chest. I felt cold darkness rise around me. Then I re-confessed my sins, just in case.

August is snuggled in his footy pajamas, lying on his back, holding his blanket beside his toddler-sized stuffed shark. He stares at me in the darkness. I can see the shine of his blinking blue eyes in the shadows of this room. I stand before a little boy who will turn two in mere hours, and I can barely run my mind through that fact. All day I've been preparing for his birthday, wrapping presents during nap time, baking a pie (blueberry, his request) for his small party at the park tomorrow evening. And all day, I've been remembering, pondering as Scripture says Mary did, the remarkable living of my son.

I sing "Great Is Thy Faithfulness," the first hymn that comes to my mouth. The old song quotes the book of James, and I remember the version of that passage I learned as a kid, about the "Father of lights" from whom every good and perfect gift is given, the God in whom there no "shadow of turning."[4]

Two years ago at this time, I was in the final stages of labor, working to push that baby out of me. This morning, after I gave him a bath, I watched my son run through the house naked, his already thinning legs powering across the wooden floor. That same body that tore out of me is now in the process of dissolving its chunky baby butt in favor of the skinny boy body. Those once fat thighs have lengthened three inches in the past month, I swear. His growing is a quiet needle in me. It pokes at the naive hope that I might keep his childhood forever. It's always slipping away, baby to boy in mere months. I cannot fathom the loss of his childhood, the reality that he will be a man one day and I will still be his mother.

"What's tomorrow, August?" my husband asked tonight while he and August played "ah-boom," their daily wrestle on the bed once Chris arrives home from work.

"Augoose two!" our little boy shouted at his daddy then giggled while Chris rubbed his prickly facial hair all over that smooth boy face.

As I sing, I watch August ease away from me into the dark, and I feel as if I am worshiping, wholly and truthfully.

> Strength for today and bright hope for tomorrow,
> Blessings all mine, with ten thousand beside.[5]

Maybe I don't know how to cling to *bright hope*, that glowing gem God placed in my chest's unsteady middle. I can't understand faith or how I've kept carrying it all these years. I can't understand what it means to bear hope with light hands, neither crushing it nor letting it float away. But I know the "blessings all mine." And sometimes I remember to lift them up. Tonight I raise my hands in the dark of August's room. I lift the hope because I cannot let it go.

25

Early July, Fifth Week of Ordinary Time

In *The Politics of the Brokenhearted*, Parker Palmer tells a story of a disciple who asks why the Torah teaches followers of Jewish law to "place these words upon your hearts."

"Why does it not tell us to place these holy words in our hearts?" the disciple asks.

The rabbi answers this way: "It is because as we are, our hearts are closed, and we cannot place the holy words in our hearts. So we place them on top of our hearts. And there they stay until one day the heart breaks and words fall in."[1]

It's summertime, but for the first time in my life, I'm freezing on the first of July. It's fifty-five degrees today and foggy. Everyone in this city acts as though this is perfectly normal. I want to shout to them that it's not okay. You don't wear coats and eat chili in the summertime! Little kids are supposed to be sweaty and sunburned and outside catching fireflies at dusk.

But I don't think most of the people here would appreciate it if I reminded them. They would probably roll their eyes and welcome me to San Francisco, where July was fifty-five degrees and foggy long before I showed up.

Sometimes I wonder how much of my spiritual life has been doused in fog this year. Maybe I need to be pulled out from the spot I'm standing in, where fog distorts my vision. Somewhere outside of this place, the sun is shining bright and hot. I just haven't found my way out of the cool mist. We've been here for almost nine months, and I'm waiting for a shift, a quick tip that will somehow turn me right side up, make me fitted for this place.

I push August in his stroller the three blocks to the playground, past the cathedral and the organic pet food store. Past the blacktop where the high school band practices during the school year.

Next week we'll travel to visit my family in Texas. We'll shed our sweaters for shorts and swimsuits, gobs of sunscreen, and bug spray.

God is whispering to me these days. *Believe*, God says. That word gets caught in the trap of my mind, but when I listen, when I'm still enough to recognize that it's there, the hard surfaces are melting away.

Believe, God is whispering. And my prayer back to God is simpler than all those prayers I've spent my life attempting. My response is this: *Okay*.

Okay, I say, pushing the stroller into the gray. A one-word prayer that marks a heart learning surrender, learning to demand less and search more for beauty than answers. *Okay, Lord.* I'm not bold enough yet for a great big *yes*. I used to pray things like "Wherever you send me, I'll go!" And then God sent me to Syracuse instead of Africa, to the city instead of the suburbs, into humility instead of impressiveness. I prayed *yes* with confidence until I realized I wasn't as strong and brave and impressive as I always thought I was.

I've been praying *okay* because it feels true.

Sometimes belief is off in the sunshine while I'm coated in fog, cold and uncertain, trapped by a sky that feels too heavy to penetrate. But hope lives here, still: God's Word on my brittle heart, full of possibility, already dripping through the cracks.

The kids on the slide are wearing winter hats, and the moms and nannies have coffee in hands. We smile at each other. August runs for the swings and shouts, "Mommy! Yet's swing! Yet's swing!"

I lift his toddler body into the black rubber seat, work to maneuver his sneaker-clad feet into the leg openings until they dangle long toward the sand. I count down from ten until his imaginary rocket blasts off. And when it does, we shout and his feet kick into the sky. I'm sure if we keep pushing, these clouds will break open and we'll find the sun behind them. We'll realize it's been there all along.

PART 6

None: Midafternoon Prayer

Wisdom.
Yielding to the Spirit.
Gratitude.

We all stand in need of healing.
We are all seeking wholeness.

—Esther de Waal

26

Mid-July, Eighth Week of Ordinary Time

I stand shin-deep in the South Platte River. I'm in Colorado with August, my parents, and my brothers' families. Chris is still in the San Francisco fog. But I am here in the river, my gaze set where the prairie collides into the mountain ahead.

Our family loves the mountains. Growing up, we were never extravagant. We didn't often get on airplanes or travel farther than our minivan could drag us. When we went on vacation, we went to New Mexico or Colorado on camping trips. We slept in tents and cooked over fires and bundled at night in our sleeping bags. We spent our days hiking or fishing. And if my brothers were fishing, I usually hovered behind them, clutching my Strawberry Shortcake fishing pole and, eventually, my grown-up fly rod, as best I could.

I've always been terrible at fly-fishing. I never really learned to tie a fly onto my leader. I still pathetically hold out my rod to my dad so he can do it for me. But I have all the gear: waders, polarized glasses, a clipper that hangs from my vest so I can trim the line, and, of course, a book pocket along the back of my vest. The book pocket has always been my most important piece of equipment. Reading beside the stream is my favorite outdoor activity.

This afternoon, while August stayed back with my mom and his cousins in the cabin, my dad took me out for an "it's been four years since you've fished" tutorial in the stream.

My cast was terrible. I was pulling my rod back far past where it should have been. The line was crumpling into a knotty mess in the water, scaring off the hungry trout. And after about ten casts, my arm ached.

It took a few minutes, but once I realized what I was doing wrong with that cast, my arm stopped complaining. The line was elegant as it unfolded over the water, landed with a silent splat, and slid downstream.

Now Dad's up the stream and my brother Brooks is two hundred feet behind me. I'm remembering the rhythm again, the grace of the arc, the fly set lightly on the top of the water and taken off again, the sound of the line slapping the surface, and the uncertain squish of my boots on the rocks. I love this feeling, the chill of river pouring past my waterproof feet, the sensation of standing still in moving water.

I'm pregnant.

I'm six weeks pregnant and no one knows. Not my dad, who just looked back at me from the beaver's dam up ahead and pointed that he's moving north along the stream. Not my brother, who five minutes ago broke into my frantic struggles with a nearby bush and helped me release the hook from the branches and retie my fly.

My husband knows. He knows I hold a delicate wisp of a life in me, something the same size as one of those fake flies my dad fashions out of string and feather.

I'm pregnant, and the world feels bright and full of possibility. The world feels dangerous and threatening toward that fleshy heart pitter-pattering inside me.

I raise my rod and cast the line out. It's beautiful. Sometimes I think fly-fishing is like praying the rosary: moving slow through each bead, letting the physical act move my unfocused body from distraction into awareness. It's the repetition, the sameness of coming to God with simple words and rhythm, that opens me to recognize the God-already-here.

I say the Jesus prayer with my cast: "Lord Jesus Christ, Son of God"; I watch the line rainbow out and plop onto the surface, "Have mercy on me, a sinner." The current pulls the line back downstream as I gather it in my left hand and raise my arm to cast again. Over and over I say it: "Lord Jesus Christ, Son of God, have mercy on me, a sinner." And over and over I watch the fly swim along the water toward me. Never once does a fish bite.

Prayer is not as hard as I make it out to be. Again and again, lift and unfold. Lay that line out, let it meander a little. Do it again. I am not profound. I am not brave in spirit. My faith is threadbare and self-consumed, but I am loved, I am loved, I am loved.

Shh, the Spirit whispers.

"Have mercy on me," I say in return.

Shh, the Spirit says again. Like a mama rocking her baby. Gentle and certain, God hushes me until my prayer is nothing but the river spilling every molecule of water from one space to another. Again and again and again, we are all moved. We are all being moved from there to here.

27

Mid-July, Ninth Week of Ordinary Time

It's been four days since August and I returned from the trip to Colorado with my family. This morning, I left him with my mom and dad for a three-day retreat four hours west of my parents' home in Texas. I haven't been to another monastery since my time at Saint Gregory's seven months ago, and this place, Our Lady of Peace Abbey in New Mexico, has a completely different feel. It's less polished here, more rustic, both in the community and in the accommodations.

This afternoon, when I pushed through the thick wooden doors at the front of an old adobe building that looks more like an elementary school than a sacred space, I'd expected the quiet, even longed for it. But monasticism is another culture. Everyone here speaks a language I barely recognize. It's *too* quiet, *too* slow. It is anti-frantic, and I love it and dread it all at the same time.

These past few days of family time have been good for August and me. I've been playing outside with my nieces and nephews, watching August dig in the dirt with my dad, and pushing down the ever-growing sense of early pregnancy nausea. I'll tell my parents about this baby when I get back to Texas. But here, alone in this monastery, I'm holding it secret for just a bit longer, eating slowly and willing myself to hold down my food, at least until we're back in San Francisco.

As I wait for dinner to begin, I stand in the bookshop beside the common room, looking at titles. A woman my age walks up beside me. I noticed her during the None service this afternoon and was surprised to see someone here who wasn't gray-headed.

She picks up the Esther de Waal book I've just been looking at and turns it over in her hands. "This one is wonderful," she says. "It's one of the first books about the Benedictines I ever read."

I look at her and smile. She's a little younger than I am, my height, a brunette with glasses in hiking sandals and a fleece jacket. "De Waal is my favorite," I say.

"Good. Me too." She puts the book back on the shelf and turns to face me. "I'm Brenda."

"I'm Micha."

"I noticed you this afternoon in the service. It's not very often I see anyone here who's anywhere close to my age."

"I was just thinking the same exact thing! This is not exactly the gathering spot for awesome twenty-somethings."

She laughs. "I've come to terms with the fact that I'm not exactly awesome." She hugs a book up to her chest. "Awesome twenty-somethings spend their summer vacations at the beach, not the monastery."

"Oh, I hear you," I say with a grin. "So I'll rephrase: This is such an amazing gathering place for non-awesome twenty-somethings!"

Brenda laughs again and turns toward the opening of the room as a middle-aged monk walks in. He's about five-foot-seven and balding. I immediately notice his social discomfort and admire him for approaching us anyway. His face is soft, and he's smiling our direction.

"Hi, Brother John," Brenda says. "How are you?"

"Fine. Glad to see you here, Brenda," he says, his voice cracking a little. He looks up at me.

"This is Micha," Brenda says. "She just got here today."

"Oh, hi Micha," he says and moves toward me. He wobbles a bit when he walks. Maybe he's in pain or maybe he's simply nervous. He looks in my eyes when I shake his hand. "I'm glad you're here," he says then pauses, looking around the room. "Oh, you're looking at some good books." He sways a bit and gazes down at the carpet in the middle of the room. "Have you read any of these books about Lectio Divina?" He looks from the floor to the bookshelves on the other side the room. "I like Basil Pennington."

"No, I haven't," I say. "But I'm interested in Lectio Divina."

"Me too!" he says and laughs.

We all stand silent for a moment staring at each other. He can't think of anything else to say. He rubs his hands together. Barbara smiles at him and is about to speak up when he remembers something.

"Would you two like to see the lake tonight after dinner, before Compline? I'm happy to take you along the trail."

"That sounds wonderful, Brother John," Brenda says. He wrings his hands and looks back down at the ground.

"Okay, okay. Well, I'll meet you back here after dinner then." He walks out of the room as silently as he entered.

"Brother John is the best thing about this place," Brenda says. "I've been here three times in the last two years, and every time I show up, he still remembers my name."

"I love that," I say, staring out of the bookshop and watching him move around the common room where two other guests are sitting. Brother John speaks to them, looking just as uncomfortable as he did with us. I think about the courage he must have to muster to approach these strangers, to live committed to hospitality despite his own discomfort. Brenda and I are silent. I look back to the bookshelves.

"How are you adjusting to the rhythm and the quiet so far?" she asks.

"It's good, but . . ." I pause and try to think of the right word. "But the silence is a little too *loud*." I smile for emphasis.

"I know. I always feel uneasy for the first twenty-four hours," she says fingering a book. She pulls it down, turns it over, and glances back up at me. "After that, I settle in."

The bell chimes, and I follow her to the dining room, where we eat dinner in silence. We sit with the two other guests and three monks around a circular table. Brenda picks up the green beans and raises her eyebrows my direction to ask if I'd like some. I nod my head yes, and she passes the platter.

The next morning, after the office of Vigils at six o'clock, we all file off for individual prayer. Even in the middle of summer, the monks are heavy coated in vestments. Here in New Mexico, summer mornings are a bit chilly. I'm in Jeans and a bright pink sweatshirt.

I follow the ten monks and four nuns out of the chapel, which reminds me more of a Baptist fellowship hall. It's white-washed and plain, far from the stunning dark-wood panels and stained glass of the small cathedral at Saint Gregory's.

We walk down the long carpeted hall, and I turn to the door that leads outside. The nuns in this community live across a small grassy area from where the guests sleep. I watch one nun walk through the grass toward her room. Everyone seems to know where to go.

I turn toward the lake and take a few awkward steps before I see an empty bench and sit down. It's beautiful this morning. The sun is bright and peeking out from behind the small mountain ahead. This is the part of New Mexico where the mountains begin, but it takes them awhile to break majestic. These are smaller, simpler: works in progress.

I've been up for an hour already and still have one more to go before breakfast or a cup of coffee. Nothing could make this moment more lovely than a hot cup of coffee. And some Ritz crackers. Crackers sound really good. I look at the small lake under the dirt and brush-covered hill, and I open my Bible to Psalm 15.

"O LORD, who shall sojourn in your tent? Who shall dwell on your holy hill?"[1] I've been trying to practice Lectio Divina lately, the concept Brother Sean mentioned last night in the bookshop. *Lectio Divina* is Latin for "sacred reading," an exercise Benedictines have used for fifteen hundred years. It's a combination of meditation and Scripture reading in which we read the Bible, not as scholarship, but as an experience of God. It's an attitude of reading expectantly, of asking, "Where are you in these words, Lord?"

One form of Lectio Divina is similar to the prayer practice Debby taught me last month. It invites us to move so slowly through the text that we're able to hear God speak one word from the passage louder than all the rest. We are to listen for that word, and when we hear it, when we see it rise to the surface, we ask God to show us what that word needs to say to our life right now.

I close my eyes and think about these words: "Who shall dwell on your holy hill?" I try not to ask, *What does this mean I have to do?* Most of my life, I've read Scripture as a call to performance. *Who shall dwell on God's holy hill? The girl who works the hardest!* My mind loves that answer. I let that tendency breeze out of me and look for God instead.

I ask again, *What do you want to say to me?* I feel a vibration near my cheek and open my eyes to find a hummingbird's beak and beady eyes directly in front of my nose.

The moment is surreal. Later, I'll remember it in slow motion: its beak coming straight for my nose, our eyes locked in on one another. I'll remember my quick scream, my arms flailing, how I threw the Bible into the grass and tripped over my own feet in a manic, wild leap.

It's only after I stand beside the bench, my arms still swinging, the tiny pink Bible crumpled in the dirt, that I register how one of my favorite creatures, that bright helicopter bird, just came to me and said hello. We *saw* each other.

I try to go back to the Psalm, but my heart is still pounding and all I can think about is the wild vibration of those motored wings against my right cheek. That hummingbird must have been terrified, accidentally coming so near to me.

I don't ever hear a word from God in Psalm 15. I sit for twenty more minutes staring at the lake, watching for the humming-bird's return, willing myself to be still, just in case she comes.

My third morning in the monastery, I sit beside Brenda and a fifty-something novice monk at breakfast, the one meal of the day when conversation is allowed. The novice monk shares his story, how he recently turned to monasticism after a failed marriage and a restored faith, and how he ended up here in New Mexico, of all places. As I force eggs down my throat despite my growing nausea and drink the decaf coffee I've been adjusting to for the past couple of weeks, I look up to find Brother Sean's small stature beside the table, refilling our cups. He reaches for mine, and moves from the regular pot of coffee in his right hand to the decaf in his left.

"Decaf, right?" he says, holding out the pot with the orange handle.

"Yes," I smile. "How'd you know?"

"Oh, I just noticed."

He doesn't know the upheaval happening to my body. He doesn't know that I am drinking decaf because my lower half is building a placenta and a human body and I don't want to bring too much caffeine into the mix. He doesn't know the depth of the secret I'm carrying inside me, the power and beauty of holding and forming a new life.

But he noticed. He noticed something so small it would probably never have occurred to anyone else to see it.

He moves to refill Brenda's cup, and I think how his hospitality seems to flow from his humility. Maybe we can't be aware of another's needs until we are quiet and still long enough to notice. Content with God's grace in the moment. *Relaxing into humility*, I say in my head. Relaxing.

Saint Benedict was really onto something. All that I long to be: the woman grateful for her life and at ease in the world, begins with allowing God into the mundane, into the earth of my life. Humility leads to hospitality because recognizing the reality of this moment—God's grace here in the present, outside the tyranny of frantic living—allows me to notice, to truly see, the needs of the people in front of me.

"You're my hero, Brother Sean," I say as he finishes refilling the cups around the table.

"Oh. Wow," he stammers. "Thank you." And he stares back toward the floor and shuffles off to the other tables, regular in his right hand, decaf in his left.

28

Mid-August, Thirteenth Week of Ordinary Time

While August takes his nap, I'm curled up under a sweatshirt blanket feeling sorry for myself. It's been three weeks since we returned from our trip, nine weeks since this pregnancy rooted itself in me. The nausea has taken over every part of my life and it feels more dramatic this time. Our mornings are marked by my constant vomiting. Last week I attempted to leave the house only to find myself deep-breathing beside August on the dirty sidewalk, trying not to spew all over the concrete.

I was just as sick the first time around. I was just as sorry for myself. But during that season of my life, the only thing I was sacrificing was my work, my feeling of control. This time there is a little boy who follows me down the hall as I run for the toilet, a little boy who stands with his back against the wall and cries while his mother throws up.

I'm sure I'm ruining him. I'm sure these days will be ingrained in his memory. I'm sure a good mom would know when the nausea is coming. A good mom would walk calmly to the bathroom, shut the door, and be sick in silence. I'm not that mom. I am walking around in a constant state of near-sickness. A few times a day it just forces itself on me, and I make a run for it.

Sometimes August brings me his blankie when I'm on my knees beside the toilet. Sometimes he hugs me. Sometimes he screams. And I don't blame him. This woman crying beside the toilet: She is not his mother. This woman on the couch, under the blanket: she is not the woman who dances with him in the living room, who build towers and recites silly poems. I don't know how to control it. I don't remember how to be grateful. I don't remember all those moments of grace last month before this constant illness took over. I'm frustrated. I'm sad.

I read Psalm 10 from my bed on the couch, hoping to will myself into gratitude. I think about my Benedictine friends in New Mexico and wonder what they're praying this afternoon. I imagine their voices chanting the words to Psalm 10 beside my own. My eyes stop where I always stop in this passage, on verse 4: ". . . In all [their] thoughts there is no room for God."[1]

When I committed to reading the Psalms all those months ago, I assigned specific Psalms to specific days of the week. I try to read this one on the tenth of every month, and every time I mouth the words, I feel conviction, a bright red laser point on my chest. God intends these words for me. I'm the one in this Psalm who can so easily make room for self-pity and worry, for guilt over what I'm not doing and what I need to do. But do I make space for God?

I lean back on the couch. I know that women all over the world have morning sickness and are still doing what they have to do. Women are sick and still trekking through well-worn paths in the heat carrying pots of water, or walking to the corporate office, or dressing children for school.

I can't focus long on the passage, so I open my laptop and check my e-mail. My inbox has a new message from a familiar name that I can't quite place. It reads:

> Hi Micha.
>
> I don't know if you remember me but we met last month at that softball game. Lily introduced us. We go to church together. Anyway, I know this may seem like it's coming out of nowhere but I'm just gonna go for it! My friends and I have a Bible study and we've been meeting for around two years, taking turns leading. But we all feel like we need to someone from the outside, wiser and in more of a position to lead. None of us really know you (at all! sorry we're so crazy!) but we've seen you and your sweet little family at church and read some of the things you've written. We're just wondering

if you'd want to lead a group of awkward and adorable twenty-four-year-olds?)

I'm sorry if this is totally weird.

Blessings,

Katherine

I laugh on the couch and read it again and again. For five minutes I don't even think about how sick I feel. I immediately forward it to Chris with a smiley face.

He writes back, "Do this as soon as possible."

I respond, "Don't you think I should at least pray about it first?"

He replies with one word: "Nope."

⊰∘⊱

A few weeks later, Katherine and her nine friends are packed into my tiny living room on a Tuesday night. I have chips and guacamole, and they've put brownies on the coffee table. I set out a teapot while August wanders around the room in his pajamas, mesmerized by the sheer number of smiling women. They ask him about his favorite toys, and he runs to his room. We hear his feet rumble down the hallway. He appears in the doorway holding "Sharky," his three-foot-long stuffed great white. He proceeds to tell the girls around him, in great detail, everything he knows about sharks, which, for my fact-obsessed two-year-old, is a lot.

"Shawks aw weelly fierce! Dey have weelly shawp teeth!"

He runs back to his room and produces his most recent library book about sharks. He shows it to Rachael and Ann and Kaili, who ask questions and laugh at his responses. I talk to Liz about law school, and Katherine fills me in about her unhappy post-culinary-school-job as a host at a fancy San Francisco restaurant. I look up to see August still talking, now about "pahcupine puffa fish" and "bat ways." The girls adore him, and I realize they probably have no families or kids in their professional twenty-something lives at all. They may need an August in their lives. He senses their kindness and absorbs the attention.

Chris stands at the door to the living room and calls August to bed. I look up, and we lock eyes for a moment. I know what he sees. He sees me: Who I used to be and who I still am. He sees the me that loves people, the me who stood in basements and talked about Jesus to sixteen-year-olds, the me who dressed as a Russian tap dancer with fire ribbons, bursting into a solo on stage for five hundred high school kids at camp. I smile back at him. *I know*, my eyes say. *I see it too.*

August pushes his way through our packed living room to give me a good-night kiss, and when his lips touch mine I feel like they might melt into my face. I am thankful. Maybe I shouldn't be leading a Bible study. Maybe I'm too messed up to lead anyone. But as I watch him walk back through the sea of twenty-something girls and grab Chris's hand at the doorway, I look around the room and think, *Jesus is answering my prayers. Jesus is leading me out of the darkness.*

Despite my churning nausea, I sit with these strangers drinking tea, avoiding the guacamole and eating my own bowl of saltines. I introduce them to the concept of Lectio Divina. We open Bibles to Psalm 19, that same passage I memorized in Africa with Janie. I say the words out loud. I repeat this ancient song of God's power and beauty in creation. My voice quivers as I read the words:

The heavens declare the glory of God;
   the skies proclaim the work of his hands.
Day after day they pour forth speech;
   night after night they reveal knowledge.
They have no speech, they use no words;
   no sound is heard from them.
Yet their voice goes out into all the earth,
   their words to the ends of the world.[2]

I say the whole passage out loud, and then I come to that last line: "May these words of my mouth and this meditation of my heart be pleasing in your sight, LORD, my Rock and my Redeemer."[3]

I finish and look up. Who am I to lead these girls? The meditation of my heart is mostly fear and doubt. But their eyes are fixed on me as if I know what to do, what to say. And then I realize: I do. I know how to choose Jesus. All along I've been choosing Jesus.

"I want you guys to sit with this passage in silence. You don't have to force anything," I say, repeating Debby's words from two months ago. "But I do want you to ask God if there's something in here for you, if there's one word God might be speaking louder than the others."

We're silent, and eventually two other girls read the passage aloud. And each time we sit with it in quiet again, asking God to point our spirits toward one good word.

I ask God, *What do you want to say to me tonight, right here? Will you use me with these girls, even though I feel like a mess?* I read the words in front of me, and I remember that belief is an invitation. I get to choose whether I live a life of faith or skepticism. I look at this room of women the same age I was eight years ago when I packed my car and arrived in Syracuse. Who do I want to be? I want to be alive. I want to be filled with bright hope. I look at the passage again:

> The decrees of the LORD are firm,
>   and all of them are righteous.
> They are more precious than gold,
>   than much pure gold;
> they are sweeter than honey,
>   than honey from the honeycomb. [4]

Honey, honey, honey. God says, *My words are like honey.* And I taste God's sweet words.

Ten minutes later we speak our words out loud. Ten women and ten stories and ten ways God speaks from a beautiful honey-mouth.

29

Late August, Fourteenth Week of Ordinary Time

On my birthday the sun is shining, and San Francisco's frigid, foggy summer is making way for warmth and blue skies. We bring the quilt my grandmother stitched us for our wedding, one soccer ball, grapes, cheese, and two books, and spread out in the grass among neighbors who've all chosen to do the same thing. People and dogs are everywhere: some girls lying in bikinis in the seventy-degree sunshine, dog owners throwing balls, shirtless guys playing ladder ball with beers in their hands. I spread out on the quilt, and watch Chris and August kick the soccer ball. I close my eyes and nap.

I wake ten minutes later to August's wet kisses. "Wake up, Mama! Wake up!"

"No, buddy." Chris says in some distorted dream-reality. "Let Mama sleep. It's her birthday. She gets to do whatever she wants."

"I want her to pay wid me! *Mama!*" My eyes spring open, and there is my boy hovering above my face, smiling. I reach with both hands, pull him down to me, and poke him in the ribs till he is giggling. Then I'm up and kicking the soccer ball.

Chris sits on the quilt and pulls out his magazine. August wants me to take him to our favorite tree in the park. The bark on the tree is rutted with deep enough crevices that we can wiggle in wood chips we find in the manicured garden nearby. We've been doing this for months every time we walk past it, and the poor tree has August-inserted wood chips sticking out on all sides. No one ever removes them. We stomp our feet past the sunbathers, the regular homeless crowd on the bench, and through the bushes. Then I squat beside August at the base of the tree.

We work in silence, decorating the trunk as if these bits of wood were beautifying it, as if our work were important and necessary.

I kneel on the ground, my hands in the dirt, and think of *humus*: earth, the root word for humility. Humility is simply being *earthed* in God, or as Esther de Waal translates it, an "exploration into reality." If we are found in God, rooted in God, we see our need and our value in the most *real* way.[1] Humility becomes a "ruthless campaign against all forms of illusion."[2]

As August's small hands work beside my own, I gaze at my fingers in the earth. I am hard on myself. So often my thoughts are unhealthy and unkind. But maybe that critical voice in my head is the furthest thing from reality. Maybe it's narcissism. I've been infatuated with the *lack* in me. And all the while God has been pointing to the *beauty*: In me. In my family. In the world.

I wiggle wood chips into place and think, *Lord, earth me in truth; earth me in Jesus.*

I am loved by God. Belief is my invitation. I am not my performance. God doesn't love me more when I'm a good mom or when I'm kind to my husband. God doesn't love me more when I take care of a friend's kid or when I say something smart. And God won't love me more when I finally figure out how to pray.

Then it dawns on me: I *am* figuring out how to pray.

∂∽∽

After I blow out the candles on Chris and August's homemade cake, I read on the couch while Chris puts our son to bed. He joins me later, holding out a cup of tea. "Happy birthday!" he toasts me with his whiskey. We clink our drinks, and he sits down. "You're not thirty anymore."

"I know. *Thank* goodness." I smile. I lie back against a pillow and prop my feet up on his lap.

"What does that mean?"

"It means I'm tired of being dramatic and young. I want to be old and wise now."

"And how do you plan on doing that?" he says, reaching toward the table to set down his glass.

"I can't tell you. It's a secret you only find out when you're thirty-one. You still have ten months to go."

"You're such a dork." He stuffs a pillow behind his head and leans back. Our couch is cranky and uncomfortable, and my husband is way too tall to relax on it. "Okay. Question," he says.

"What one thing do you want to accomplish before you turn thirty-two?"

"Ooh. Deep thoughts!" I pause and think. "Um, I want to give birth to a baby and feed it milk and keep it alive."

"Okay, okay. Good goal." He laughs.

"And I want to be wholehearted."

"Micha, that's not a goal. Goals have to be concrete. You can't just say some vague word and say it's your goal."

"It's my birthday! I can have an abstract goal if I want to. And I want to be wholehearted."

"Okay. It's your birthday. You're allowed." He rubs my right foot. "So, tell me, how are you going to be 'wholehearted' by this time next year?"

"I don't know. I'll figure it out." I smirk and take a sip of tea. One of our pastors, Chuck, is a therapist who has this way of approaching Scripture with such gentleness. In one of his recent sermons, Chuck quoted from a book called *Crossing the Unknown Sea*: "The antidote to exhaustion is not necessarily rest. The antidote to exhaustion is *wholeheartedness*."[3] I can't remember what passage of Scripture Chuck was talking about in that sermon, but I remember how he explained wholeheartedness as "allowing every part of us to be loved by God." He said that to live wholly we must learn to love the Lord with *all* our heart.

To love with all my heart is to have a heart that is undivided. It is to be the Real Micha, my truest self. The Real Micha is not ruled by fear or guilt or anxiety. I want to give my full attention to my need for Jesus, my full attention to the reality that God's grace is present right here, in my life.

I sit up a little and say, "Okay, so here's my concrete goal: I want to figure out how to see Christ in all the small, everyday moments. I want to notice God at work. Because I talk about how I believe God is restoring me and the people around me. And restoring the whole world. But I've lived most of my life forgetting to pay attention."

"So you want to learn to pay attention?"

"Yeah," I smile. "Wholeheartedness. I will be the Lady Who Pays Attention," I lean back against the pillow.

"Okay, Lady Who Pays Attention, do you need more cake?"

"Nope, I need more foot rub."

"Done. Then I will be the Man Who Rubs the Feet."

30

Mid-September, Seventeenth Week of Ordinary Time

In the Celtic Christian tradition, where every act of daily routine had an accompanied prayer—milking the cow, hammering a board, getting on and off a boat—the woman of the home blessed her house and family each night as she banked the fire of the hearth before bed. This was a prayer of protection over her husband and children. This was a reminder that the Trinity lived and moved among an ordinary mother doing the most mundane of daily tasks.

Esther de Waal describes this prayer in her book *The Celtic Way of Prayer*. The woman would spread the embers "evenly on the hearth in the middle of the floor," forming them into a "raised heap in the middle." Then she would divide that heap into three sections, laying down peat between each section in the name of the God of Life, the God of Peace, and the God of Grace. "The circle," de Waal says, "would then be covered over with ashes sufficient to subdue but not extinguish the flame in

the name of the Three of Light." Then the woman would stretch
her hand out over those ashes and speak this prayer:

The sacred Three
To save
To shield,
To surround
The hearth,
The house,
The household,
This eve,
This night,
Oh! this eve
This night,
And every night,
Each single night.
Amen[1]

I clean the kitchen tonight, scrubbing the stove where olive
oil splattered when I pan-seared the pork loin two hours ago.
My husband is putting August to bed. I can hear Chris singing
"Sweet Baby James" in the other room, the song his dad always
sang to him.

August's favorite part is the beginning, when Chris sings
about the cowboy who lives alone among the horse and cattle.
Chris holds a note, his tone lilting into the next line.

I'm quiet, listening to my husband's untrained voice and
unconsciously moving the sponge to his rhythm. The days are
getting shorter now. Evening has arrived outside my kitchen
window, and I stop to stare at the gray cement wall of the building

beside ours. I set down the sponge and lean back against the open doorframe that leads into the dining room. I take a good look at this tiny kitchen where I've spent these eleven months, making and cleaning, putting away and pulling out. The repeated chores have become a litany of grown-up tasks. This tiny little kitchen with its terra-cotta tiles and twelve-by-twelve inches of cream Formica counter space. I will miss this apartment, but I will not miss its kitchen.

We move in twelve days. After doing our best to stay, digging through the city laws to secure our rights as tenants, we've come to this standstill. Our landlord can kick us out. And he is going to. Once we realized that there was nothing more we could do, August and I went on a two-week tour of apartments, across this town and even over the bridge. Here in San Francisco, places turn over so quickly, I knew I'd have only two weeks to find our next home. One week in, we walked into a beautiful place with hardwood floors and two (two!) bathrooms, a washer and dryer, and, glory of glories, easy street parking. I applied for the apartment that day, and we were accepted the next.

We're leaving North Beach, which means that much of our life here will change. We've tried to build community around the playground and the families at the library toddler time. And I know those relationships probably won't survive our move across town.

The dining room is already full of boxes. All week, I've been packing and sorting and thinking, *Didn't I just do this?* And it's true. I did just do this.

I pick up the sponge again and step past the boxes to the dining room table, wipe it down. Chris is still singing in the other room:

And goodnight moonlight lady,
rock a bye, sweet baby James.[2]

In the thirty-first chapter of the rule, Saint Benedict states something so remarkable that I keep coming back to it each night as I stack bowls and dry plates. He says, "All the utensils of the monastery and in fact everything that belongs to the monastery should be cared for as though they were the sacred vessels of the altar."

All the utensils.

I take the sponge and rinse it in the silver sink. Nothing in this skinny kitchen is all that special. And I've been living as if my tasks as a mom, those daily, mundane tasks—the brushing of my son's teeth, the wiping of his bottom, the dressing of his body, the kissing of his scraped knees, the soothing of his wild terrors—as if they were nothing significant, as if they were simply normal, what every mother does.

I'm mesmerized by Saint Benedict's words, that the monks should care for every tool in the monastery, from the garden hoe to the kitchen cleaver, as if it were the very chalice of the Eucharist, the tool that brings the blood of Christ to the lips of believers.

I am undone.

I'm not sure why I've been waiting for this. I'm not sure why I needed someone to say it to me this way. But with Benedict's words, I feel my world has been reborn holy. Suddenly my life, all these small daily instruments I am packing in my home, and the very sippy cup I fill with milk and raise to my boy's lips, is an instrument of worship.

How did I miss it before? How was I so sure that God did not value my unimpressive daily life?

I see my reflection in the dark night window. My short hair is bobby-pinned out of my face. My red sweatshirt hangs loose from my chest. And in the reflection of the glass pane, I see it.

I am a priest. I am a priest of the gospel, holding the chalice to the lips of my son. Carrying the plate of bread to the hungry. My life has value because God has touched every mundane moment with the glow of holiness. It matters. It all matters.

Chris closes August's door with a quiet click. He walks the ten feet to where I stand in the middle of my kitchen, entranced by the power of my mysterious, glorious everyday life.

"What are you doing?" he says in the quiet voice we use when August is asleep.

I wake from my trance and turn to him in the doorway. "I'm thinking about this prayer Celtic women used to recite when they prepared the family hearth for nighttime." I smile, aware that I'm becoming a "prayer nerd," if ever such a thing has existed.

He doesn't ask why anymore. He's used to my tangents. He knows all about the Celtic prayer book I've been reading at night and underlining with the ferocious passion of a girl in love.

"What's the prayer?" he asks, still standing in the doorway, the soft light of the stove's lamp and the darkness behind him give him a warm glow. He's part icon.

"It's a prayer for protection, for a family. For a home. A wife would pray it while she made the mark of the Trinity in the ashes of the day's fire," I say. "I think it's so beautiful."

I look at Chris for his confirmation and give him grace for not living in my head and knowing exactly why it is "so beautiful."

I keep going. "I was just wishing I had a hearth where I could pray for you guys every night before bed. Where I could make the mark of the Trinity."

He grins. "Well, then. You'll have to find one." Then he turns, walks back into the darkness. "You coming?" His voice trails off down the hall. Of course an ancient mother would need to pray over her hearth, over the place she bakes the family bread and where the little hands come to warm themselves early in winter mornings. It's also the place she probably most feared. The place where fire brought warmth and sustenance but also the possibility of danger and destruction. The hearth is the place of life and the place of dread. And only a woman's mind could hold the complexity of such a thing as she cooked and tended the fire and shooed the babies away.

With my sponge I wipe a line from the northern tip of the stove down to my gut where the first signs of my baby are taking shape, that small firm roundness. Then I lift the sponge and sweep it across, left to right. As I do it, I whisper, "This night, / And every night / Each single night."

PART 7

Vespers:
Evening Prayers

Grace and mystery.
Peace and awareness.

And we are put on earth, a little space, that we
learn to bear the beams of love.

—William Blake

31

Early November, Twenty-Fourth Week of Ordinary Time

I'm five months pregnant, and I'm still throwing up. Not as often, but just as dramatically.

Last month, August followed me into the bathroom and was so angry he slammed the toilet lid on my head over and over while I continued to vomit. Sometimes I feel we're surviving, like we're turning a corner, like he may not be permanently scarred by this pregnancy, and then he slams the toilet lid on my head, both of us sobbing, both of us wiping our faces and starting over again.

We are one month into our new home. August's room has wall-to-wall carpet and a window that faces a street always packed full of interesting events. We're near a hospital so the fire trucks zoom down Divisadero day and night, and he's learning to sleep through the wild blare of the engines. He's transitioned to a big boy bed, and he and Chris have room to build amazing tunnels and spaceships out of the mass of cardboard boxes left behind from our move. Most importantly, this apartment has a big, beautiful bathtub, and my pregnant body is grateful.

Today I'm on my knees again in the bathroom, and August is standing in his spot in the hallway. This time he yells, "Don't worry, Mommy! I'll help you!" He runs off and, thirty seconds later, arrives with his blanket and wraps it around my shoulders. I lift my face to his, tears in both our eyes. Can we keep living this way every day?

"Thank you for Buppy," I say.

He touches my face with his pointer finger, part poke, part caress. "Now let's go play cars, Mama."

Okay. Let's go play cars.

32

Early November, Twenty-Fifth Week of Ordinary Time

It's a Tuesday morning. I drive along the bay through the Marina after dropping August off at his preschool, where he continues to go twice a week even though it's now a ten-minute drive instead of a five-minute walk.

I adjust my shoulders in the car (even *they* feel pregnant) as I pass a dozen or so spandex-clad women running behind super-strollers along the bay. The sun is bright and sparkling the water. No fog over the Golden Gate today, only the burnt red of it against a green mountain.

What will Debby and I even talk about? I think as I turn the car into my spiritual director's parking lot. *She's going to ask me how I am, and I don't know. I'm tired. I've got pregnant-brain. I'm feeling All the Feelings. But I'm fine. I'm fine.*

I'm five minutes late. I sit on the flowered pastel love seat. My growing belly almost brushes the tops of my thighs.

"How are you?" she asks.

"I'm tired," I say and smile. Then I sigh. "I haven't slept much lately, and this pregnancy is so exhausting. But, you know . . ." I look up at Debby. I stop my words. I don't know what I was going to say anyway. *I'm normal*, I think. Some days I'm "paying attention" and noticing God and loving the people around me with patience and kindness. And some days I'm fiery with August and back to my old ways of inner-self-bashing and praying like a frantic yapping puppy. Last week, while my not-even-two-and-a-half-year-old screamed and pounded the floor when it was time to dress for school, I threw his clothes at him and yelled, "Dress yourself!"

Since moving into our new apartment, I've added "administrator" for a local parachurch ministry to my title of stay-at-home mom, in hopes of a little extra cash. I hoped I'd use the money to pay for more childcare so I can write more often. But I didn't really think it through. Those ten hours of administrative work each week are only keeping me from time with August, and I'm still writing late at night when I should be sleeping. Plus, I've just been commissioned by a church to write five poems for the Advent season. And for some reason, I can't seem to stop throwing up.

"What do you mean when you say you're tired?" Debby asks.

Words fall out of me. "Why can't August actually sleep during nap time? Why can't I get out of bed before August does so I can pray? Why can't I write the book I want to write?" Under all these words is a stabbing acknowledgment of failure: I ought to be able to do more with my life than just live with a two-year-old.

There it is: the *lack* in me. I was doing so much better for a while. I was starting to believe that God loved me, that my life had value in all of its mundane ritual. And now I feel trapped again. I'm still trying to earn my value by a string of deserving points.

"Is God disappointed in me?" I ask Debby.

I used to stand up and preach that transformation was possible. I was the minister. I wept when I read Scripture out loud, when I told high school kids that Jesus was real and he loved them. Now I look at myself and see a striver: always doing and never living up to whatever expectation I've set for myself. Was I only confident in Jesus back then because I felt like I

VESPERS: EVENING PRAYERS

was good enough? Because my life was bigger than the park and the library and the toys and the meals and the hugs and songs? Do I really believe God loves my unimpressive mother-life as much as God loves when the hungry are fed? When the slaves are rescued? When life-changing words are spoken to the crowds? I'm not convinced.

I stop speaking, wipe my eyes. Debby sits across from me. She's silent. We stare at each other for at least thirty seconds.

"I think we should pray," she says. I let my head fall forward. *Every head bowed and every eye closed.* "Micha, I want you to ask God what he has for you in this. In this exhaustion."

Every time we meet together, I wait for Debby's disappointment. I wait for her encouragement to work harder, do better, pray longer. Each time I think the lecture is about to come, she asks me to pray instead.

I set my hands in my lap and turn my palms to the ceiling. I want God to love me. I want to believe God loves me. I want a swoosh of Spirit in here. I want a word spoken in my ear that says I'm enough. I want God to understand that I'm human and frail. I want to know I'm not a failure: The girl who didn't go to Africa. The girl who didn't stay in ministry.

I beg God. *Here I am,* I say. *What do you want to say to me in my exhaustion?*

I hear Debby's voice. She's far away, an echo in a forest. "Micha, God wants you to know that you are not a horse. You are not a horse attached by the neck to a carriage. And Jesus is not the master in the seat of that cart. He is not whipping you when you stop. He is not screaming at you, hooking you into a hard harness, despising you for your pace. You are not the horse, and Jesus is not the carriage driver."

175

I wipe my eyes. I take long, slow breaths. *You are not the horse*, Jesus says. *You are not the horse.*

I hear Jesus say the words. And I turn around to look at him. He stands beside me, in front of the carriage. He holds the harness, the thick leather and metal collar. He waits to lift it from my neck. I look at Jesus. I look in his eyes and I recognize his face, not because I've seen it before. It's not the face from the Sunday school pictures. I know this face because I recognize the warmth of his nearness, how soft the air is when he's standing beside me. I felt it that first time I walked down the aisle as a seven-year-old and asked him to rescue me. I felt it in my bed all those childhood nights when I begged him to make me saved *enough*. Even in my fear of God, Jesus was my comfort. He has always been my comfort.

Okay, I pray. *Okay, Jesus.* The harness slides off smooth.

Debby's voice comes back. "Jesus is asking you to sit beside him in the carriage. That's all, Micha. Jesus is asking you to sit beside him. Sit beside him and tell him why you're tired."

I stand in mud, ankle deep, and turn around to the carriage where Jesus now sits. He pats the bench beside him. I walk to him and climb up. We gaze at each other. He looks at my protruding belly and smiles at my face. He glances at my belly again. *It's good to see you here,* he says. *It's so good to see you.*

33

Early November, Twenty-Fifth Week of Ordinary Time

The girls named our Bible study Yoobs. Originally, in the days before we started meeting in my home, when they couldn't come up with a name, they called themselves "Unnamed Bible

Study." Then they shortened it to UBS until UBS became Yoobs, which I think is hysterical. I think they are hysterical.

We've been studying the books of First and Second Timothy, letters from Paul to his young protégé in the far-back pages of the New Testament. We took a vote and decided we liked the idea of studying something meant for the young, for this young pastor learning how to care for a community of new believers caught up in the story of Jesus. I want that to be us: young and caught up in the story of Jesus.

After three months of meeting together every Sunday night, we've made it to the end of Second Timothy, where Paul expresses some final thoughts to the young man who has been like a son to him. These words are some of Paul's most memorable. They're about persevering in faith, whatever it requires.

I have fought the good fight, I have finished the race, I have kept the faith, the always eloquent Paul says as he looks toward a fairly certain looming death.[1]

"What does it mean to *keep* our faith?" I ask the girls who are spread out on the mustard brown couch and the floor of the apartment. We've grown a bit in the last few months. There are now fourteen of us crowded around the coffee table. Thankfully this new apartment has a bigger living area than the last one, or there's no way our whole crowd could be sitting here.

"What does it mean to keep the faith?" I ask again, thinking about *keeping* like it's something you do inside yourself. The same way you *keep* a secret. *Keep* a memory. Paul says keeping faith is an action. He throws out these metaphors. Fight. Race. As if faith were simply a choice to continue. A choice to stand up when the opponent flattens you. A choice to keep running, one foot after another.

I look around the room to see if anyone else is seeing that word *keep* as well. Liz speaks up. "You guys know this has been a hard few months for me." Some of us nod. She's been recovering from a relationship that had ended by the time I met her last summer. "I've never felt like faith was something I had to hold on to—like something I could lose—until lately. It was always there before, you know? And now. Now it feels so unstable. I read this and think how much I want to hold on." Her voice breaks when she says it.

Last week, Liz sat on August's bedroom floor while he played around us. She told me how her ex-boyfriend left her feeling broken. How she can't seem to recover. And how his crumbling faith led her to question her own.

"I don't know what to do with my doubt, Micha," she said. "I'm not this person. My faith has always been so strong. I'm so mad at myself."

Liz is in law school. Her bus stop is a block from my house. She had texted me on her way home that day and asked what I was doing.

"Making a dinosaur puzzle. Waiting for someone awesome to stop by," I'd written back with a smiley face.

That day I leaned against August's dresser and watched him carry his favorite rocket book over to Liz and drop it in her lap. "Wead dis," he said.

"Aug," I said. "How do you ask?"

"Peas."

Liz opened it and read the whole book aloud. I watched them and thought about her words. What did I need when I first began to question my faith? *God,* I prayed in my mind, *what does she need?*

She finished. "Again!" August demanded.

"Not right now, August," I said. "Miss Liz and Mommy are talking." He looked up at her and threw the book onto the bed then dragged over his basket of blocks. Liz began pulling them out and stacking them.

"Liz," I said, "God's not mad at you. Even if you are."

Her eyes met mine, and her hands rolled the blue wooden block up and down between her palms. "God's not mad at you. And all your questions? I figure if God didn't want us asking questions, he wouldn't have made everything so freaking mysterious." I raised my eyebrows, and she smiled.

"Do you really think so?"

"I think you can torment yourself inside your own head or you can bring the thoughts into the light of day. Sometimes if you get them out of you and into prayer, they look different. They look a lot more hopeful."

She nodded her head and stacked the blue block onto the tower.

"Hey, Liz?" She looked up at me, tears in her eyes. "There's enough hope, even for people like us."

࿓

Now, as she admits her doubts to everyone at Yoobs, I see how much courage it's taken her. She doesn't want to be unsure. She's organized, responsible, a natural leader. She wants to have it all together. She wants to *fight the good fight. Finish the race.* She looks around the room at her friends and waits for someone to respond.

It's silent for a while. Then I speak. "When I read this and thought about 'keeping' my faith, I thought about how when someone is ordained a Benedictine monk or a nun, they go through this long period of training where they live like a monk. Like a two-year internship. They practice celibacy, they live at the monastery, and they pray a trillion times a day before they make the vow that they'll do it for the rest of their lives."

I look around the room. Cecelia got a job with Google right out of college two years ago. She's smart and gentle and has been dating the same guy since high school. And she struggles with anxiety the same way I do. She just started therapy for the first time in her life, and she already seems more confident. Caitlin is recovering from the end of her on-again, off-again eight-year dating relationship. It's been challenging and emotional and freeing for her. She's trying to figure out how to be what her friends are calling "Caitlin 2.0."

There's Molly and Ann and Kaili and Rachael. All around me these women are looking to me, asking me to tell them how to do this one monumental thing. *Believe.*

Do I know how to believe?

"When they make their vow," I continue, "they come before the altar and recite all the traditional things you'd expect. They commit to obedience and lifelong conversion and stability. They're giving up their rights to have sex or a family or a regular job or their own home. They put all their trust in God's willingness to take their small vow and make it into a life that matters. And then, at the end of the ceremony, they do this thing I think all Christians ought to be doing—or at least talking about—more often. They essentially say, *I'm trusting you with this. Don't screw this up for me, God.*"

I open my Bible to the middle, where I've marked the line in the Psalm Benedict instructed all novices to recite when they commit to the monastic life: "Sustain me as you have promised, that I may live; Do not disappoint me in my hope."[2]

When I sit before these girls and teach, I am brave. I am a

believer. And the things I say aloud feel true in the fullest sense. How is it so much easier to preach a merciful God to these women than to myself? Maybe even that is an act of grace. When I speak it aloud and believe it for them, I'm learning to hold out mercy for myself as well. I'm learning to *keep* this faith.

I catch Liz's eye across the room. "I think somebody forgot to tell us we can say this to God as well: 'I'm giving you my whole life, Jesus! Don't disappoint me in my hope.' I love that even the monks—even the most faithful—can ask God to follow through on his promises.

"So I've started praying that too: 'I'm giving you my life: this delicate, beautiful thing. Please don't disappoint me, God.' Most days I have to choose to believe that I really do have hope. And that God holds it.

"Maybe faith is a choice. More than anything else."

Liz wipes her eyes, and Rachael reaches over and puts a hand on her back. "We love you, Lizasaur," Katherine says from her spot across the coffee table from Liz. We're quiet for a minute, all of us looking at our cups or at each other.

Kaili wipes her eyes and breaks the silence. "Seriously, Micha. Do you ever read books that *aren't* about monks?"

I gasp and then throw my commentary of First and Second Timothy at her. "Yes! See? *Paul for Everyone*! There is not one single monk in the whole thing!"[3]

"Not impressed!" Kaili yells back. We laugh, and Caitlin gets up to find more brownies.

34

Mid-November, Twenty-Sixth Week of Ordinary Time

It's Saturday morning. I sit on the couch in my pajamas at ten thirty, thinking of all the work I should be doing: for my administrative job, around the house, on my poems. I need to stand up, but I feel glued here. Maybe *glued* is not the word. I feel swallowed here. The air weighs more than I do. I'm overwhelmed by the options, so deep in the pile of to-dos I can't touch anything on my list.

My breath shortens. My heart pounds. I think, *I can't live like this*. Everything feels too spacious and too tight at the same time. I lay my head on the couch cushion.

August runs into the room. "Let's read a story!"

"Okay. Go get one," I say. "And then sit here with me, and we'll read it." I try to smile. How will he remember me in twenty years? How will he remember my anxiety and my exhaustion? What will he tell his therapist?

My husband is in a great mood. He made pancakes for breakfast, and he's cleaning up, listening to the news in the other room. He calls to me: "We should do something fun today! It's beautiful. Let's go to the park!"

I'm immediately infuriated by his words. Who is he to think that just because he doesn't work on Saturdays that I don't as well? I work full time as stay-at-home mom. Then I do this administrative work on the side. I've been commissioned to write those Advent poems that will never be good enough that anyone should pay me for them. Then I'm making (*making!*) a baby inside my body. I'm tired. I'm frustrated that he gets to leave the house every morning five days in a row and have some magical life in the office, where people don't poop on him and scream at him. People have conversations with him and they eat meals at restaurants and he listens to music while he walks to a tall building and looks out the window at a beautiful city.

I go on and on in my head. It's amazing how quickly I can turn against this man I love.

I hear myself talking. My voice is frantic. "I know *I* can't go to the park, Chris. I have to work on these poems that are horrible and get the newsletters mailed out. It was a stupid decision to think that I could do either of those things, much less both at the same time. But you haven't seemed to notice."

August is here with his *Thomas the Tank Engine* book. I've read it fifty-three times this week, and I cannot do it again. He lies down beside me on the couch, and I take a deep breath and begin to read but stop two pages in. "I really shouldn't be reading this right now, you know," I say in the tone I save especially for Chris. This is his job. He should be reading this book. He should know that I'm exhausted and I've read this fifty-three times this week and if he really cared about me and my pregnancy he would give me a break every once in a while. Forget that he's cleaning the kitchen while I sit on the couch. Forget that he made breakfast for us thirty minutes ago. I breathe the heat in my throat. The walls press in, threatening to squeeze until I'm flattened into the nothing I already feel.

Chris is snapped out of his happy cleaning. "Fine," he says and walks across the open room, from kitchen to living area, and grabs the book from my hand. "Why don't you get out of here? Since you can't stand to read this book. Since everything in your life is so awful."

"Really?" I say. I stand up from the couch, and Chris takes my seat beside our son. *Really* is all I can say. What I want to say is, *Why don't you just say it? Why don't you just call me crazy, and we'll get it out there?*

But I don't. I go to our room. I run a bath. If I were a teenager without a belly protruding five inches, I would bury my face in a pillow and angry-cry until someone came to rescue me. Instead, the hormones surge, and I inch into the water. I have nothing to pray so I make myself say the Jesus Prayer. I hiccup while I form the words. I slow my breath to their rhythm.

> *Lord Jesus Christ have mercy on me, a sinner.*
> *Lord Jesus Christ have mercy on me.*
> *Lord Jesus Christ have mercy.*
> *Lord Jesus Christ.*
> *Lord Jesus.*
> *Lord.*

By the time I get to the end of the prayer, my body is shaking. "Lord, Lord, Lord," I say, remembering Jesus beside me in the carriage. Remembering that grace eases me out of the harness and lets me sit beside my Savior on the bench. *Lord, Lord, Lord.*

Our house is dirty. We moved here six weeks ago, and we still don't have pictures on the wall. *Lord Jesus Christ have mercy,* I say to that thought.

Breathe in Jesus, breathe out Christ.

My husband arrives at the bathroom door, tea in his hand. He hands it me.

"I'm crazy, Chris," I say, looking up at him, ashamed and tired. "Like, actually insane. And mean."

His eyes crease and his lips stay closed tight. I know he's worried.

"I'm sorry," I say.

"I know." He kneels down beside the tub. He touches my hair and kisses my forehead. "I know, honey."

"Thank you for the tea," I say. He leaves the bathroom.

I hold my cup and sit as long as the water will let me, watching my toes on the faucet, thinking of hope and redemption and what it might mean to be healed of a mind that hates me.

I dry off. I dress myself. I leave the poems and the administrative work in my computer, and join my husband and son for a trip to the park. We walk down the building's carpeted stairs and out into the city. Chris pushes August in his tricycle, the red helmet with the smiling racecar framing my boy's tender head.

Chris was right. It's a beautiful day outside, sun on our faces. I'm not myself, still swirling inside, still aching for relief from whatever it is that squeezes my brain until it refuses to process the good. But here, in the sunshine, I sit on the grass and watch my husband and son play volcano. They run up the hill until it "explodes," then roll down it giggling, screaming, "Ouch! Ouch! Ouch!"

Again and again they climb, then fall, then laugh and start again.

35

Late November, Twenty-Seventh Week of Ordinary Time

On Tuesday morning I make a list for our groceries. And, then, under that, I write out some of the good things in my life. I write:

A husband who brings me tea and makes pancakes.
A boy who is obsessed with stories and rockets.
A baby who swishes around my insides and makes me want to eat pickles.
A chance to write poems for some people who actually want to read them.
Hot baths.

I set down my pen and slice an apple for August to take to preschool. I throw a cheese stick into his Thomas backpack along with it.

"It's time to go, buddy!" I yell to the boy in his room at the train table. "Let's brush your teeth and get your shoes on!"

We make it out the door and pass a couple in the building's hallway. August says, "Hey, guys!" — his new greeting for all the neighbors. We walk out our building's door and up the hill to where we're parked a street over.

We listen to Veggie Tales sing all the way, and we scream, "Whee!" when we *whoosh* down the hill on Franklin.

"Mama, dis is our fastest hill! And when we get to school, I'll pay twains and see Miss Jenny and show her my vo-cano book."

"And what do you think she'll say about your volcano book?"

"She'll say, 'Voooocaaaaanoooooes!'"

I turn and head up Filbert. Up and up until we teeter on the edge of a paved abyss two blocks from school. When the car noses down the steepest hill in town, my foot on the brake, something good rivers across my chest. All the true things take their rightful place in my mind.

Goodness, the sky whispers. *Goodness*, the road says as I walk across it holding my boy's hand. *Goodness*, says the laminate floor in the one-room school. August settles beside "Sookie," his favorite girl. He shows her his book.

36

Late November, Last Day of Ordinary Time

It's Saturday morning, the day before the first Sunday of Advent. Chris takes August to the park so I can spend a couple of hours revising the last of the five poems I was commissioned to write. The first of them will be read tomorrow in a worship service at a church in Seattle. It's a poem about the annunciation and the actual spiritual act of the incarnation. Mary is taken from her simple dirt floor into the expanse of heaven and impregnated with Jesus. It's a little risqué, and I love it.

Its first stanza has been on my mind all day:

After the angel dissolved, I stood among the skies,
no longer clothed in brown linen, but with fire:
the sun's silk my gown. I leaned into the swirl of gold and lit.

I sit in a coffee shop and try to write about pregnancy and the glory of bearing new life and offering it to the world, *leaning into the swirl of gold* and being *lit*. I feel like Mary, aware that I carry a pearl in me, something fashioned in another, holier place. Most of the time, pregnancy feels frustrating, like an illness. My body is rarely happy with what this child is doing to me. But there are moments that are mystical, as if the incandescent glows beneath my skin and I can barely hold it for fear of being burned.

There are seasons to pregnancy: There's the grueling first season of carving out room in one's body for the child. The second season of nourishment and energy. And, of course, the final season of ripeness, of expansion, until the child forces its way out. The body gives in to the weight of all the *holy*.

I like the idea that Advent is like pregnancy, that Advent is a preparation of our hearts for the entering of Jesus into the world. I like the idea that we eventually give in to Jesus. Of course we fight it. We want control of our own destinies. We want to worship the thing that feels most comfortable or most urgent.

But when Jesus arrives, he opens a world to us in which comfort is far less important than beauty, in which urgency is replaced by grace. Advent is the season when we get to practice making room for God to enter into our world, in all its need, in all its strange beauty.

Perhaps in this season of preparation, I can make room for both the beauty and the ache, both the noise and the silence, both the making and the being made.

37

Late December, The Second Day of Christmas

It's our second week of Christmas travels, and the three of us drive the Jersey Turnpike, a two-hour stretch from my mother-in-law's in Philadelphia to my father-in-law's in Connecticut.

I am pregnant with another boy, a fact that gave me a huge sigh of relief when I heard it on the doctor's ultrasound table. As much as I would love a little girl, I understand boys. They're wild but simple. And they roar and jump and always land on their knees for no apparent reason. I'm dreaming about how sweet it will be to watch August wrestle his brother on the couch. I imagine how I'll put a stop to all that wrestling. I'll lecture that *it's not safe* while secretly adoring it for the same reason. I also have a recurring daydream of my handsomely strong college-aged boys walking in the door for Christmas break. They're funny and sensitive and excited for a homemade meal, and they can't help but kiss me on the cheek while I'm stirring a pot on the stove. (Yes, I'm a romantic. Who can blame me?)

Being pregnant is terrible and remarkable and wonderful. And this experience of pregnancy can sometimes feel entirely separate from the actual baby I will hold and love and feed. It felt this way with August as well, impossible that I wouldn't be pregnant forever.

Of all people, a mom of a very alive and needy two-year-old ought to be able to remember that pregnancies lead to Real Live Children. But it still feels unfathomable that this baby will be *another son*, an entirely new person. And he will belong to us, to our family.

I turn around in the car and ask a squirmy August questions, hoping to keep him distracted from his boredom. We chat about the baby, how it's moving in my tummy now, but soon it will come out and August will finally be a big brother.

"Aug," I say, "what should we name your brother?" Chris and I have spent the past twenty minutes of the car ride talking names, weighing the ones we really like. I've been agonizing over how each choice will probably determine our baby's entire character. *That name will turn him into a jerk! If we call him that he'll be totally lazy!*

August barely thinks before he blurts out, "T-Rexy!" and, of course, Chris and I laugh and think our child is the most adorable and clever creature to ever walk the earth.

August, however, doesn't get the joke. He thinks he's just named his baby. He continues the conversation about my pregnancy, only now with the assumption that our child has been appropriately named after his favorite dinosaur.

"Mama, why is T-Rexy gonna cry sometimes?"

"Is T-Rexy just a sweet baby?"

"Can I show T-Rexy my blankie?"

I can't stand how sweet this conversation is. So I keep it going. "Do you think T-Rexy will look like you, August?"

"No! He looks like a dinosaur!"

Of course he does. His name is T-Rexy. What was I thinking?

I turn my face back to the landscape of New Jersey, a few barren farms but mostly the backsides of strip malls and travel stops. We pass the Newark airport and the old landfill where once all the trash from New York City was buried, day after day for decades. And then we come to an industrial complex, another blight on the land, where coal is burned and its dirty smoke puffs up into the sky. Right now, it's nothing more than a series of smokestacks and metal piping, steel cutting across what would have been some nice countryside on the outskirts of New York.

But I've seen this place in the night, when the steel pipes are lit with small orbs glowing white, placed strategically every two feet across the long planks of metal. At night, it looks like a tiny city lit for a party. It looks like a castle of light.

⧉

It was night when Chris and I passed that complex on our first road trip together after two months of romance via long e-mails and longer phone conversations. We hadn't even kissed each other yet when we went on that trip to New York.

I met Chris in early November and didn't see him again until the weekend in mid-January when we finally made something official of our impassioned e-mail writing. The weekend he visited me in Syracuse, we talked for hours, as if all the twenty-something years we'd spent apart had been a terrible mistake and we had to frantically catch up. We ordered pizza and, of course, both loved pepperoni and black olives. (*What?* No one *likes pepperoni* and *black olives!*) We played football with friends in the snow, and he tackled me and held me down a little longer than acceptable.

And then, alone in my apartment, on my red-and-white-checked couch, he'd taken my hand in his, his thumb moving slow across the curve of my skin, when I felt blood rush out of my nose. I screamed and ran hysterically to the bathroom where I held a tissue to my nose, assuring myself that nose bleeding must be the least sexy of all physical ailments. I looked up to find him at bathroom door, grinning. I rolled my eyes and assured him that this happened to me all the time. He shouldn't start thinking he was special just because my nose bled when *he* held my hand.

"I know," he'd said. "You do this for all the guys."

By that next weekend we were in the small beginnings of love, where everything lines up, your humor and your common adoration of pickles and cottage cheese. We both understood the other's passion for literature and our young, budding frustrations with the evangelical church. And everything that did not match was equally fascinating. Chris's mind was breathtaking. He spoke with passion about Russian literature and that moment when Kitty ice skates with Levin in *Anna Karenina*. I was smitten.

It was the next weekend when we passed that industrial complex on a Friday night, en route to his dad's house in Greenwich. We were twenty-two and twenty-three years old. We both wanted nothing more than to know the other, to be known by the other.

We moved past the coal plant alongside the Jersey Turnpike, and Chris said, "I always think this is the most beautiful part of the drive to New York." I turned toward him and stared at the shadowed profile of this boy I hardly knew, so moved that he could see the glowing New York skyline up ahead and still call this collection of towers and puffs of smoke—metal piping lit with plain rough round light bulbs—beautiful. And it was. It was beautiful.

In the car that night, I told Chris about the place I came from. I told him about the flatness of Amarillo and how in high school when I was feeling like I most needed to hear God's voice I would throw my backpack into my Chevy's back seat and drive due west until I passed every road in town. And there, right behind the very last strip mall, sat all the land.

And that land went straight to the edge of the earth. "Land so flat you can see the earth curve," PawPaw said once.

I'd pull my car to the side of the dirt road and climb onto the hood. I'd lean back against the front window and watch the sun slip out of view. I told Chris I never prayed as well as when I watched the sun leave and had nothing to say to God at all.

"One day," I said, "I'll take you to Amarillo. And when you get there, you'll look out the window of the plane and see hundreds of flat square miles of brown and yellow land. And you'll want to say it's unimpressive and ordinary. This treeless town with straight-lined streets." I touched his hand on the stick shift. "But if you say that, I'll never forgive you."

"Never?"

"Never. I said you'd be tempted, but I didn't say you'd be allowed to say it. If you say it, you'll be wrong." I paused. "Not to mention the biggest snob of all time."

"Well, I definitely don't want to be the biggest snob of all time."

"Yeah, I know." I said. "You're at least a little lower on the snob spectrum."

"A little. Barely."

We drove toward his dad's house, where we would share our first kiss in the basement, like two teenagers, making out when the parents are asleep upstairs.

"Chris, I know this is totally dramatic. But when I think about my hometown, I think about how the land is so bare that all you notice is the sky. I think how sometimes the beautiful thing is what's not there, more than what is."

And we passed the small coal plant, his hand on the gearshift, my hand on his.

☙❦

By the time we're on the George Washington Bridge, August is asleep and I've closed my eyes. I feel the sun heating the window, even though it's thirty-four degrees outside. My husband drives straight across the Hudson River and into the city, and I keep my eyes closed because I've seen it before. We've made this trip so many times. We curve the road until we join another highway, this one to take us past the Bronx and into Westchester County. I watch our progress in my head.

I think about this baby. It's true what they say about second children getting the raw end of the deal. I kept a journal when I was pregnant with August. I recorded every movement and change in my body and in his. And this baby has been living in the midst of my thinking about everything else. I wonder if there's something beautiful about that too. That in the middle of all the wild of my life, the exhaustion, the sadness, the busyness of raising a kid and writing, this child has been growing and flourishing and arriving at life. It's ordinary, yes. But it is also a miracle when something meticulously formed arrives out of chaos. I open my eyes to see the sun streaking through the window and onto my husband's hair. Are we prepared for this?

Do we know how to be parents to a kid who isn't August? Why do I feel even less capable of being a mom than I did the first time around? By now I should be bold and ready. But each year of mothering keeps revealing how little I understand of how to do this.

I reach up to my husband's hair and touch the place where the light is shining.

"T-Rexy," I say. "Not a bad name."

He laughs, still looking straight ahead out the window. "Nope. Not a bad name at all."

PART 8

Compline: Night Prayer

Resolution.
Quietness of the soul.
Trust.

And if tonight my soul may find her peace, and sink in
good oblivion . . .
then I have been dipped again in God, and
new-created.

—D. H. Lawrence

38

Early March, Ash Wednesday

Our new apartment is walking distance from church. Tonight Chris has a work dinner, and once again August and I are making the trek to the Ash Wednesday service without him.

It's dark, and I'm huge, thirty-nine weeks pregnant. I push August in the stroller down Divisadero. Our neighborhood is referred to as NOPA (North of the Panhandle), an area of town that is slowly gentrifying. We're on the edge, where NOPA hits Western Addition. If August and I head east from our home, we walk past the matching blue government-housing apartments. Across the street is the Buddhist monastery, where the scent of incense is a constant presence. It wafts through us as we pass the two beautiful dragon sculptures along its elaborate facade. Monks smile at us in their red and yellow robes.

This area is different than living in North Beach where, despite typical city fears and discomforts, we felt like part of a community. We felt safe, known. Here there are different faces every time we're at the playground. Here the librarian doesn't recognize us when we arrive or remember August's book passion du jour.

But we can walk to church. And that has been a sweet addition to life in our new home. August and I hike the five blocks together on Wednesday mornings for Moms' Group, and on Sundays we share the commute as a family. After church on Sundays, we keep walking several more blocks past our building to the farmers' market on Oak Street, where we pick up veggies or something yummy for lunch and take it to Alamo Square Park for a picnic and an incredible view of the city.

I don't feel secure here at night. At night people pace the sidewalks without anywhere to go. Sometimes I hear screaming across the street. After the sun goes down, August and I rarely leave home. But tonight he and I are brave. I push the stroller down the sidewalk at 6:50, making our way to Ash Wednesday. And as we go, August is telling me a story about Angelina Ballerina and a scary rat. I'm saying, "Whoa!" and, "That's cool!" but really, my mind is far away. I'm annoyed Chris isn't here with me. I'm worried about this baby coming soon.

T-Rexy is due in one week, which means I will not be denying myself anything during Lent. There is no Lenten fast that can demand as much as a newborn baby asks of his mother. I'm prepared for the sleeplessness and the breastfeeding, for the exhaustion. What I don't know is how I will mother two kids at the same time. *How will I play with August while I feed my baby? What if I can't get T-Rexy to sleep when August sleeps and I never read another book the rest of my life?*

When I'm not worrying about the future of life with two kids, I worry about childbirth. I worry about labor and its uncertainty. Then I switch and worry about August. Lately his tantrums have become intense and frightening. He's two years and nine months old and can swing from sweetness to violent surges of anger in a moment. And when he enters the wild-eyed rage, I feel like everything is out of control. All I want is to know how to help him. But he can't understand himself, and I can't understand him either. He screams and slams his body around for twenty minutes, and eventually I either scream back or cry while I watch him throw himself on the ground.

Maybe his tantrums aren't normal. Maybe he's one of those "strong-willed children" people write books about. I don't really understand what those things mean or what a "normal" two-year-old's tantrums should look like. I'm scared of disciplining too much, and I'm scared of disciplining too little. I'm tired and I haven't even had this baby yet. I want someone to come into my life and tell me I won't ruin my kids. I want someone to say, *These are things you're doing right. These are the things you're doing wrong.* As it is, I feel like I'm flailing. At the end of the good days, I think I'm the greatest. On the bad days, I'm sure my lack of wisdom will wound my son forever. There must be a balance somewhere.

I guess it's appropriate I should feel this fragile on Ash Wednesday, a day for recognizing our own frailty. I may miss the mark with my kid. Despite good intentions, he may not receive from me what he most needs in his childhood simply because I'm busy giving him what *I* think he needs. Parenting is frightening that way.

The beauty of Ash Wednesday, though, is not the ashes on the forehead, the reminder of our frailties and failures. It is the shape of the ashes, the cross, with all its wild, illogical demands. It calls us to recognize how our lives are flashing and fading. It asks us to notice our need for restoration, our longing for eternity. The cross is the hope that all I'm missing right now—everything I'm not being for my son, whose needs I'm only beginning to scratch the surface of understanding—is all gathered up in mercy. Grace is poured over our ashes, a cold cup of clear water washing away the gray goop on our faces, taking our weak-willed offerings and remaking them beautiful.

Maybe redemption is the only possible story my life is telling.

I drop August off in the nursery. Another year, another Ash Wednesday alone. This time I sit in the balcony, five minutes late. But this year is different. From my perch up high, along the side of room, I notice the faces of people I know and love. One year later, I feel like I'm part of this place, woven into the stories of the people in this room. I see the family wading through the long process of adoption, the couple in their midthirties who have just begun to date, a few of the Yoobs girls sitting together.

This church is mine now. And I still have a long way to go. What will Lent hold for me? It's possible that T-Rexy will be six weeks old by the time Easter announces itself. A six-week-old baby can reach and grab hold of things, focus his eyes, smile at his mom and dad.

I forgot about the first baby smile! God, I've been so afraid that I forgot about the first baby smile! I sing this in my head in the middle of all the prayers of confession and renewal. I forgot about the joy.

It's coming before Easter. It's coming, despite all my fear.

I stream down the stairs in a line of fellow travelers. Easter is coming to all of us. But first, we have to hold the ashes. First the hard truth. Then the magic.

I meet my pastor in the front of the room. I look in his eyes when he says, "Micha, you are from dust, and to dust you will return." And I know. I feel the ashes pressed into the pores of my forehead, and I see it with clarity. *I am ashes. And Jesus is the Phoenix that rises from my ruins.*

৵৽৽

When I get to the nursery to pick up August, I watch his face flash from happiness to confusion. The ashes on my head are anything but subtle. I was toward the end of the line, following behind a few hundred souls who were marked with the cross before me. All that forehead grease has given my ashen cross a look more akin to ink. It takes up the whole space of my forehead.

"What's on your head, Mommy?" August stands and drops a ball from his hand. He walks toward me, singularly focused on my forehead, where something is definitely not right.

"It's a cross, buddy," I say. "It reminds me that Jesus loves me."

"Oh," he says and reaches up to feel it. He pulls his hand away and looks down at his pointer finger, now coated in black grime.

"Look!" he shouts, pointing to another woman gathering her little boys at the same time, "That mommy has one too!"

We walk home the five blocks in the dark of evening. This time, I'm calmer. This time, I'm not as afraid of the dark. I'm aware of how rare it is for both of us to be together out in the nighttime. The air is cool but clear. The moon glows down on us, and when I can't understand what August is saying from his position in the stroller, I stop and walk around to face him. I lean close to hear his voice.

"What were you saying, buddy?" I ask.

He can't remember. Once he sees my face again, he says, "It's still there! Your cwost is still there!"

When we make it back to our apartment, I squat my awkward body down to remove his shoes.

"We've gotta get your jammies on and brush your teeth and only two stories tonight," I say as I pull off his second sneaker. As I speak, my son touches the cross on my forehead again, gentle, with one careful finger.

"You're beautiful, Mommy."

I look at him, and my eyes fill. Here we are, alone in the entryway of our apartment, both of us staring at the other, and

I feel his love for me, his hope for me. I believe he wants my wholeness as much as I want it for him. We may spend our lives misunderstanding each other in so many important ways. But he'll remember that I loved him. He'll remember that sometimes, for a brief, remarkable moment, we *noticed* one another.

I see him. He sees me. His beautiful mama. I am his beautiful mama.

❧❦

My pastor once said that Jesus will not transform our lives until we see him as beautiful, not simply useful. It's the loving him that changes us, my pastor said. Not the using.

As I lie down in bed on Ash Wednesday, the black mark wiped from my forehead, I position myself in the most comfortable pose. My unborn baby gets his own pillow, and I lie on my left side, staring in the dark at the wall.

Chris is beside me, talking about his day and his long work dinner. He asks, "What did you love most about the service tonight?"

"You know, I think just having time alone," I say. "Getting to sing alone and close my eyes awhile. There's something about that service that's always so magical to me."

"It's because you love sad things," he says.

I laugh. "Sad, *beautiful* things," I correct him.

"Exactly."

I tell him about August saying I was beautiful and how I've been wondering whether I love Jesus or simply use him.

"Micha, I'm sure it's both. I'm sure you have moments of genuine loving and moments of using. Like any other relationship."

"Yeah. I guess," I say.

"Maybe the process of growing deeper in faith is really just learning how to find Jesus beautiful more often. Learning to notice when you *are* using him."

Chris leans over and kisses my temple.

"Good night," I say, then stare at the shadows on our wall. The streetlights shine in through our tall window across the room.

Maybe if I looked for the beauty more often, I'd discover prayer there, in the looking. Maybe prayer *is* the looking. All those passages in Scripture about seeking the Lord. "Seek, and you will find," Jesus said.[1] I've always thought seeking God meant spending a lot of time with my Bible and praying long, organized prayers. Prayers that made me feel something. Prayers that spoke the names of all the sick people and all the lonely.

I've spent my life hoping I would one day be whole enough to pray the right way. But the truth is, prayer is the very thing that makes me whole. Seeking, it turns out, is sometimes a messy, unimpressive life of loving, then using, then loving again.

I turn my body to the right side and heave myself and my baby—those extra thirty pounds around my middle—to face my husband in the bed. I grunt and readjust the pillow on the right side. Then, after all that work, I snuggle my face into Chris's arm.

Relationships are messy, I think. *Who am I to think I would one day accomplish prayer? Have I accomplished marriage? Have I accomplished motherhood?* Chris tucks my hair behind my ear, and sleep folds over me.

39

Mid-March, First Week of Lent

I've been so tired these last few weeks of pregnancy that I

haven't found the energy to get out of bed before August wakes each morning. But today, maybe because my mom is here and I have a psychological need to make sure the coffee is ready for her waking, I'm staring at the ceiling at six thirty when Chris gets in the shower. I sit up and waddle out of bed.

My due date was three days ago. I'm in the long waiting. Yesterday, when the store clerk asked when I was due, I mustered a brave smile and said, "Two days ago! Ha!" And when the cashier gasped and collected herself, I noticed her wild gaze at my body and knew I'd stare too. I don't look human. My ripeness is near-offensive.

I've already done everything I scheduled on the calendar. There are no more dinners planned with friends. My administrative work has been tidied up and passed along to the woman taking my place. And now my mom is here during her spring break, waiting out the long, aimless days with August and me, walking up and down sidewalks in hopes that all our walking will shake T-Rexy loose.

I put on my robe and shuffle down the hall. Spring has been revealing herself these past couple of weeks, and the sun is shining brighter and bigger every morning. I stand alone beside our bay window and its third-floor view and watch the sun lift up over the roofs of the city. I hold my breath as the tops of all those buildings are brushed with gold. The effect lasts only a minute, but it's remarkable.

"Good morning, Jesus," I whisper. Then my litany: "Oh, Lord, open my lips, and my mouth will declare your praise."

This is Lauds. This is the hour of awakening. "Satisfy us in the morning with your steadfast love, that we may rejoice and be glad all our days," Psalm 90 says.[1] It sounds so gentle of God to want to satisfy me. In my younger years, I confused the word *satisfy* with *sanctify*. Back then, when faith was easier and my questions were quieter, *sanctified* seemed like something I could live up to. I needed to "be holy, as God is holy,"[2] and then I'd finally earn my shot at God's kindness. If I could be sanctified, then I would finally be at peace. I read books about pursuing holiness as if it were a race I was running. As if I would arrive. As if one day I'd be enough.

This morning, I stand before the window, watching gold drip across the city, and recognize that all along, in spite of my ordinary striving and my half-hearted faith, in spite of the wild thumping of my brain against its skull, God has been dripping gold on me, dripping gold on everything around me—*satisfying*.

Sanctify means to set apart, to be *made* holy. Sanctify is when God hovers over the unimpressive loaf of bread, the bottle of table wine, and transforms them into Eucharist. Sanctify is when God gathers something mundane, something everyday, and hallows it. God feeds us bread, and it drips with honey in our mouths. The Spirit of God is the one who does the sanctifying. Never once, *never once*, has that been my job. My job has been to seek, to look, to stand at the window under the great golden sky and say, "Here I am. Ready to be remade."

All this time, as I pushed August on the swings and talked to moms at the park, as we colored and as I sliced apples, all I wanted was to find prayer. In reality, God was finding *me*, here, in my everyday. I was being found.

At the window, before my mother walks into the living room and August charges from his bed, before I stretch my aching back in downward dog on the yoga mat in the living room, hoping my water will break and send me hobbling to the hospital, and even as I finish this first cup of coffee, God is whispering, *I am making you new, Micha. I am satisfying you.*

So that's grace, I think. Grace and holiness are both the first page and the last page of the story. We are always being found by God. And if we pay attention, we recognize God's good gifts. We gather them, look closely at them, and lift them to the golden sky.

40

Mid-March, First Week of Lent

The contractions start. We eat breakfast and make plans for the day, and I feel one, heavy and rolling through my middle. It takes my breath. I stand beside the sink in the kitchen and stare at the wall, where I've tacked a Czeslaw Milosz poem on a piece of printer paper.

> Don't run anymore. Quiet. How softly it rains
> On the roofs of the city.[1]

The words fade into a blur of ink. And then I'm back in the world again. My mom notices my gasp. I turn toward her and smile. "Let's hope there are more of those," I say.

"Guess we'd better go for a walk, then."

And that's what we do. We pack the diaper bag and walk down the stairs to the sidewalk outside our building and decide we'll push the stroller eight blocks to the grocery store, for no reason.

"Surely we need something," I say. What we really need are hills and movement. We need my body to churn and tide. We need that terrifying wave to roll through me again and again until it forces a life into the world.

Another contraction comes on that walk. And then another thirty minutes later. By lunch they're every twenty minutes. By afternoon, I check my bag and add anything I need to its contents. I double-check for the baby's coming-home outfit. I call Chris at work.

"Is it happening?"

"Probably. I think so. Yes."

When I put August down for his nap, I tell him a story about T-Rexy, who comes into the world with rescuer super powers, just like his big brother. Late at night, while Mommy and Daddy are asleep, August and T-Rexy wake to a shining light in the sky, a symbol calling the Super Brothers to strap on their jet packs and blast out into the night. They fly over San Francisco, following the glowing light until they reach a tree where a kitten is trapped. They swoop in! T-Rexy holds the branches back while August grabs the creature and sets it in the arms of its terrified owner. Then, before anyone can praise them or even see their faces in the darkness, the Super Brothers rocket back into the sky and home into their bedroom window. They lie still as Mommy comes in to check on them in the night. She never even knows.

"August," I whisper, as his eyes get heavy, "Mommy will probably go to the hospital to have T-Rexy soon."

"Okay, Mama."

"Will you listen to JoJo? Will you be brave while we're gone?"

"Mm-hm," he says.

"The Lord bless you and keep you," I whisper. "The Lord make his face shine on you and be gracious to you," I move my thumb down and across his forehead, an invisible cross. "The

Lord turn his face toward you and give you peace."[2]

❧

I sit on my bed and try to read as the contractions come quicker and quicker. It's been eight minutes since the last one. My mom is in the other room, and Chris is on his way home. I'm not supposed to call the doctor until they're six minutes apart. So I try to pray. I open the Bible and laugh when it falls open to Psalm 15:

> O LORD, who shall sojourn in your tent?
> Who shall dwell on your holy hill?[3]

It's the Psalm I was reading last summer at the monastery when the hummingbird appeared and beady-stared into my eyes.

"Okay, God," I say. "I'm paying attention."

The wave rolls through my body, and I stand with my hands on the bed, breathing long and deep while the force grows wide in me. *It's almost like God*, I think, afterward: *wild and dangerous and making everything new.*

41

Mid March, First Week of Lent

When T-Rexy explodes into the bright, cold world, he doesn't look like a dinosaur. He looks like his brother: round features, wisps of brown hair on his head. He's heavy, long-torsoed, with skinny piano-playing fingers.

He screams at the entry from flesh into open air, but that very wailing demands his breath. This is his first lesson in living.

Only in those tears do his lungs contract to gulp oxygen. By the time his cries cease, he's already learned to live.

He comes to me, and we hold each other, my skin his first incubator. I let him work for his milk, rooting around my chest to find his way there. He smells me and I whisper to him, and he recognizes the voice of his mother, his glassy eyes working hard to find my face. It's all miraculous, how this new human finds his way around, grunting and squirming until he arrives at my breast. He fights for that first gulp of milk and learns to swallow, right there in my arms.

The sun pauses in the sky that March morning. We stare at each other, and I hold him against my skin. Chris touches our son's head, and I look to my husband, who moves to stroke my hair as well.

"You did it," he says. "You did it again."

We name our second-born son after his two second-born uncles, both kind and clever, talented and silly. It seems fitting: Brooks Andrew.

And in the glow of post-birth euphoria, I feel unafraid. I feel brave and powerful. I feel like the water must have felt when Jesus changed it to blood red wine.

42

April, Lent and Eastertide

The weeks that follow are a haze of comings and goings: my mother in town, then Chris's mother. Meals dropped off and friends cradling my baby on the mustard brown couch, touching his features with delicate fingers. Those weeks are already a blur of photos: August holding his brother with an anxious adult hand hovering near the baby's head. A baby swaddled tight on the stripes of the bedspread, his eyes wide and uncertain at the flash of the camera. There's the proud daddy, bouncing the crying infant, the tired mother dreamy-faced and slow.

There's the weekend when I'm infected and I shake under the covers and Chris brings the baby to me and I work and work to keep the milk coming. There's the tender breaking when I'm sure I can't do this. I can't love two children at once when both need all of me at all times. There are tears in the bedroom and prayers in the rocking chair while I feed our son and Chris or my mother-in-law plays with August in the other room.

The days begin and end with tiny metal cars slamming into one another on the floor of August's room, where I sit cross-legged, a baby in my arms gulping my milk. I make the brown tow truck talk in my best impression of PawPaw's accent as I sneak glances at the four-week-old in my lap.

It is all too much. Too much growing and too much wonder at these children who came from me. Too much rage inside my older son who tantrums and thrashes every day, screaming at the world. Too much sweetness, too much fear.

Sometime in the midst of all those foggy days, my spiritual director sends me an e-mail. I'd apologized to her for failing to hold to some commitment. I'd cited my exhaustion, my struggle to adjust to all the changes. Her e-mail says: "Micha, please try to remember not to be so ferocious with yourself."

When I read the e-mail to Chris, he says, "You should write that in lipstick on the bathroom mirror."

Ferocious. A dinosaur word. When we're ferocious with ourselves we're more likely to be ferocious with the tenderest ones around us, roaring and stomping and demanding our own way, never stopping to see the fear in the little boy's eyes or the fear in our own. My family has entered the unknown: a sensitive boy learning to share his mom and dad, a new baby learning to live in this world. And, I'm just trying to remember to wash my hair and brush my teeth. I write, "Don't be so ferocious with yourself" in crayon on a piece of construction paper and tape it above the kitchen sink.

43

Mid-May, Fourth Sunday of Easter

I love my church but hate that we use those tiny plastic Communion cups, the ones that look like tumblers for dolls. The more that liturgy and tradition and mystery have crept into my faith, the more I want one big, fat chalice. I want to drink from the same cup as everyone else worshiping beside me. I want the pastor to hold that cup out to all of us and force us into community, germs and all. I want the old and the young, the weak and the strong, the fearful and the brave, to press their lips to the same curved edge and drink.

As it is, we all trickle forward, receive our baby cups then sit back down and swallow at the same time. I find the practice lacking in grit.

It's Sunday and I'm in the balcony, where Chris and I have taken to sitting these days, what with all the baby-shushing, standing, and rocking.

August is in Sunday school, and I've just returned from the "mothers' room," where I've breastfed and burped my little two-month-old bundle. I hand Brooksie over to Chris, who places him gently into our "manly" baby carrier, the one that looks like a front-facing black-and-tan backpack. Our baby's all plump with milk and falls asleep to the gentle thump of his dad's heartbeat. I spend the next few minutes staring at my bare arms, wondering how long it's been since they were empty.

Now my left hand holds the wine-filled Communion cup, and my right pinches a tiny circular wafer. We're waiting for the room to gather their miniature meals, waiting for the minister to declare, "This is Christ's body, given to you. This is the cup of salvation."

My eyes close, and I think about the prayer my pastor prayed earlier in the service. He said, "Lord, heal us of our small ambitions." I have no idea what else was said in this service. My mind is fuzzy with exhaustion and distraction. And those twenty minutes I spent in the back room breastfeeding are already a blur to me, even though a speaker fills the air there with the sounds of the sermon.

All I can remember is that prayer from earlier in the service. *Small ambitions.* All I can think about is that my small ambitions might need healing. *Healing is such a gentle word*, I think to myself. *Such a kind word.*

In a rare moment of quiet prayer the other day, I reopened Saint Benedict's Rule. It had been awhile since those long afternoon nap times pre-pregnancy when I drank tea and thought long about my monkish mothering. I miss those days, when I prayed. And even then, it didn't feel like I prayed. Even then, it didn't feel like I had time to read. And now, I'm jealous of my discontented former self.

I reread Chapter 72, the portion of the rule where Benedict is winding down, where he's making sure his monks understand what he's been trying to say all along. These are his last words in the rule, which he began writing in around AD 530 but continued to revise until his death, which some say occurred in the year 547.[1]

"It is easy to recognize the bitter spirit of wickedness which creates a barrier to God's grace and opens the way to the evil of hell. But equally there is a good spirit which frees us from evil ways and brings us closer to God and eternal life. It is this latter spirit that all who follow the monastic way of life should strive to cultivate, spurred on by fervent love."[2]

I hold the bread and wine and consider the "bitter spirit," how often I let my fear and skepticism scream louder than the gentle voice of grace. And I remember that other word, *cultivate*. I want to cultivate, to dig and till, to *earth* myself in God.

I have spent my life performing for people, for God, for myself. I have begged for a grander story than the small, beautiful life I've been given. Yet still, even in the longing for a more impressive existence, my ambitions have been too small. I wanted to save the world. But God wanted me to see how he was already saving it. God was already writing the Big Story, and my part was to watch it unfold. If only I could notice, then I'd recognize myself being saved alongside the children I never rescued. I'd recognize that I am as desperate as they. Our stories are all *being told* in the Great Story. We are all being written together by a generous Author.

My story is here in that bigger story, the story of a God who comes to the fainthearted, the bored, the bitter-spirited, the ones who cannot prove themselves worthy. I have spent so much life clutching tightly to the bitter spirit, keeping the gate of God's grace closed tight. I have worked hard but denied myself the mystery of grace. And here I sit in San Francisco, a city I barely considered three years ago, taking Communion with a roomful of people I never imagined I'd one day share my life with.

The pastor says, "This is my body, given for you. Do this in remembrance of me."[3] And I chew that bread, moving the tiny wafer from side to side in my mouth because I need Christ to touch every part of me. I need Christ to pass through my milk to my baby. My mind is too tired for prayers made of words. *Let this be my prayer, God.*

My life is small, but God's ambitions are bigger and wider and deeper than anything I planned or meant my life to be. I choose this. I choose to cultivate a life of the Spirit, to cultivate grace in the potty training, in the tantrums, in the *relentless sameness* of my plain, ordinary, beautiful life.[4]

I drink the wine. Chris, drinks his too, but awkwardly. He can't get the cup to tip all the way back with the baby strapped to his chest. He hands it to me, almost emptied. "Finish it for me?" he whispers.

I take his wine and gulp it down.

44

Late May, Fifth Week of Easter

Change comes quick. First there's the phone call, then the interview, the callbacks, the two weeks of uncertain waiting. And when my husband gets a job offer from the dream company, he calls me the moment he's off the line with them.

"Do it!" I say.

"Yes, ma'am."

He takes the job, and we order Shanghai dumplings and I "Woot!" when he comes through the front door and August dances around the kitchen because I turn on the party music and in the swirl of the spinning, Chris says, "They're giving us the choice."

I stop. "The choice of what?"

"To stay here or go to Austin," he says. "Either office has room for me."

We have a weekend to decide. A weekend. Do we choose this community we've only begun to love, this city where we've built friendships that matter, that could really matter for years to come? Do we stay in this cool, foggy world where we pray and drink Communion from tiny plastic cups and where everyone lives in small apartments and sprawls on sunny days in bright green parks?

Or do we choose my home state? The ground my great-grandparents farmed, where highways lead straight to my family? I have dear friends from college in Austin. We could afford a house with a garage. We could grow a garden, and maybe August would stop screaming at the sight of bugs.

That night Chris and I lie in bed holding hands and staring straight up at the ceiling. "Would we be giving up if we leave this place," I ask my husband, "just as we were making a home here, just as it was becoming ours?"

Chris sighs. "The bigger question is whether or not I'll be booed out of Texas."

"It's Austin," I laugh. "They have a much lower standard for burliness. And there are a ton of food trucks."

I smile at the thought of my husband, *my husband*, making a home in the state of Texas. My baby-wearing, cocktail-perfecting, tennis-playing, legs-crossing man who would prefer to discuss his current obsession with Napoleon's adviser, Talleyrand, than the engine of some dude's truck.

"Chris. Can I do this again?" I am sick at the thought of picking up and starting over again with an almost-three-month-old, an almost-three-year-old, and a delicate sanity.

"I think the question is really whether we can *not* take this chance to be near your parents. Do we stay here, far from both our families, or do whatever we can to be near yours?"

We both know, there in the dark, when Chris asks God to make the choice clear, that it's already clear. It just hurts.

Amazingly, miraculously, it hurts.

45

Late June, Second Week of Ordinary Time

When the movers stomp into our apartment, I drive August to his best buddy Alton's house where they have plans to play all day before saying good-bye for too long. *Too long. Probably forever*, I think, as I drive the car south through the city, staring hard at every rainbow flag, every park and hill. The sun is shining. The fog has lifted, and every house is planted side by side in a tidy row, glimmering in the morning sun. I try to remember how it looks. I want to remember that it was real, that once, for almost two years, I lived in this place and fell in love with its golden light, its fog-coated strangeness.

I find a spot in front of Alton's house and unbuckle August from his seat before heading to the side of the car where Brooksie has been gazing out the window, awake and aware to something only he knows. August stands on the sidewalk, and Alton runs out of his house. "August! August!" he yells, standing behind his chain-link gate. I pull Brooksie out of his car seat, and his body flops gently into mine. He's holding his head up now, so I lift him to my left shoulder, where he can stare seriously at the blue sky and the shiny green leaves and the pastel houses braided tight in their spots on the land.

When we get inside, the older boys take off toward the toys in the back of the house, and Alton's mom, Katie, and I talk. I don't really have much time to stay. Katie offers me coffee, and I turn it down. We both had baby boys just months ago, and we lay them down side by side on the floor of her kitchen and snap pictures.

"Why didn't we take more pictures of them together?" I ask her. But we both know the answer. We were tired. And overwhelmed. And we didn't know it was all going to change. *Too soon. Probably forever.*

I look at my friend standing in her kitchen offering me coffee, and I'm thankful. I hold that sweetness up to God with a quick breath: *Two babies side by side on the kitchen floor, August squealing with his best buddy in the back bedroom, a friend who loves me.*

I sigh out loud. "Too bad we won't get to spread these babies out on your kitchen floor every month," I joke. "This should really be a regular thing."

Katie laughs. "Well, you can always stay, you know." She cocks her head to one side and grins.

Four weeks ago, during that brief weekend of choosing to stay or go, I stood in her kitchen, in this very spot, and she tried to convince me to stay. "We'll be a community together," she said. "We'll take care of each other . . . Think of all the families at our church choosing to live in the city, to raise our kids in the city. We can do this together."

I listened to her then, taking in her words, knowing I didn't really have a choice. If we had the chance to be near my family, I'd never forgive myself for turning it down. I had to choose them.

I look at her now and smile. The kind of sad smile that says, *I know. I know I'm choosing something else.* There are tears in our eyes. I break the silence by grabbing my keys off the kitchen table. "I promised Chris I'd be back to oversee the kitchen stuff."

I add, "Don't even try to say good-bye yet. We'll deal with that later, okay?" I find August, who can barely look up from the train set to my face. "I'll be back later this afternoon. Listen to Ms. Katie and have fun! When you come home, everything will be on the moving truck!"

I gather my baby from his place on the floor, and we walk to the door. I take the four steps down from her house and turn around.

"Katie, you're a superstar." I pause. "Thanks."

"I'd say, 'Anytime,' but, you know . . . ," she says from her front stoop as I walk out the gate and toward the car.

I roll my eyes as dramatically as possible. "You're never going to let this go?"

"Never."

I snap Brooksie into his seat. When I drive away I honk my good-bye like some small-town old man passing a friend on Main Street.

༄྅

I go the long way home, through North Beach, while Brooksie sleeps in the back seat. I drive past our old apartment, and I think about that time in Amarillo when my childhood friend Sarah said God would plant roots in the ground, that they'd follow August and me through this city, along the sidewalks, breaking open the ground to make room for life. I drive down our old stroller path, past the cathedral and the pet store and the apartment where the tiny old Chinese man always squatted outside his front door smoking in the shadows.

I drive and cry and finally turn the car toward the middle of town, where we've lived for the past nine months. The home where my second baby started his small life.

When I get to our street, the moving truck is blocking a large mass of parking spots in front of our building. I leave the car a couple of blocks away and carry Brooksie down the hill and past the men tugging all my things up the metal ramp.

I've only been gone for an hour and a half, and the apartment has been transformed. The dining room is empty. In the kitchen, two men are moving quick hands over our dishes, rolling them up, scratching out words on boxes.

Chris is standing there, writing something down for the movers.

"Hey," I say after I set Brooksie, asleep in his car seat, in the corner of the living room. I try to speak louder than the constant hum of shuffling paper and folding cardboard and stomping men-feet. "I guess you didn't need me for the kitchen?"

"Yeah, I can't believe how fast they are."

We're used to moving, but this is our first time to have movers pack our house. We're both shocked by the speed and wonder of this new concept.

Chris runs out to pick up some sandwiches, and I hover around the movers, answering questions and sometimes staring out the bay window in the living room.

Sunday night I finished my last study with the Yoobs in this now empty room. We spent the past three weeks talking about *kaleo*, Greek for "called." It was a study designed by my spiritual director, Debby. The first week she included these words from Elizabeth O'Connor: "[The] call was to come to most of us through the ordinary events of life, which were to be extraordinary because we brought to them a new quality of asking and listening."[1]

While we talked about discovering our individual skills and passions, I couldn't help but keep coming back to the truth of that statement. *Kaleo* arrives in the ordinary, and God makes it miraculous. We talked about wholeheartedness, the possibility that what God wants most of me is my full surrender in the everyday moments, my whole being opened wide for the filling.

There's so much more I wanted to tell them. I didn't plan to leave so soon. *Probably forever.*

☙❧

Two weekends ago, we had a good-bye dinner with friends, and I borrowed a dress from the shared closet in the house where some of the Yoobs live. The movers are finishing and I have nothing to do and there's nowhere for Brooksie to spread out, so after Chris and I eat, after I nurse my baby in some awkward floor space away from the all-male moving team, I swaddle him in the baby wrap and set the borrowed dress in a bag. Of course I would forget until my last day in this city to take the dress back to my friends.

Caitlin and Katherine are home on this Saturday afternoon. I text on my way over, and they promise they'll stick around. I already said good-bye to them at our going-away party last night. So this reunion is a surprise, and they're excited to see Brooksie awake.

When they let us in, I stick the freshly dry-cleaned dress in Katherine's closet and unwrap Brooksie so both can get one last snuggle with my baby. We sit on the couch for a few minutes, and I fill them in on the movers' status and our plans for flying out of town. While Caitlin holds Brooks, he poops. Loudly. And I immediately see that his pants are wet.

We laugh. Then I groan. "Nooo. You guys. I didn't even bring a bag with me! I walked thirty minutes away and didn't even bring a diaper. What is wrong with me?"

"Um. I think you're allowed to be a little distracted today," Katherine says. "We'll figure it out, girl."

So we do. We spread his baby body out on the countertop and clean him with wet paper towels, laughing hysterically. Caitlin brings forth a beautiful golden kitchen towel from Pottery Barn, and I beg them to think of something different. Surely there's a trashy towel somewhere in this apartment. But no, we wrap the pretty towel around his fleshy bottom half. I pull the headband off my head and stretch it around my baby's waist. Caitlin snaps pictures with her phone of all of us smiling beside our sadly diapered baby.

"Please tell the Internet I apologize for being the worst mom of all time," I groan. And Brooksie smiles at the ladies, happy for all the giggles and attention, still lying on his back, his legs kicking the air like he's running a race straight up and out of this apartment.

It's too cold to go pantless, so his wet pants go back on, and I feel the damp warmth of him across my middle when his body falls back into mine. The girls walk me to the front door, and we hug one last good-bye. I promise to mail the towel back to them.

"As if we want it!" Caitlin laughs.

"I'll wash it in hot water! I promise." I shout from the sidewalk.

Then I look at them for a long moment and wave another good-bye. I walk out into the chilly sunshine, and Brooksie quiets despite his wet body. He leans his head against my chest, and I sigh.

There's never a moment when you learn how to be whole, just like there's never a moment when you learn how to be a mom, or how to see the holy around you. There's only practice. There's only noticing. There's only the constant prayer that your heart would become what God is making it to be, that you might lift your eyes from the ground where the city is all cement and metal and danger, and toward the warm sun, which burns till the fog flees back across the expanse of the wide sky, beyond the tips of the great buildings.

I pass a small alley, marked with the street sign that says "Austin." I laugh. *Austin*, it says. *One way*. I pull out my phone and take a picture. And I remember it's midafternoon. The monks are praying None, what Macrina Wiederkehr calls "the Wisdom Hour." She says this is the hour when we prepare ourselves for the coming evening, when we learn surrender, when we remember our own aging, our own impermanence on this terrible and beautiful and living planet.[2]

This is the hour when I say good-bye to San Francisco. This is the hour when I walk slowly with my three-months-alive child curled against me in the breezy June. Nothing is perfect, my child wet and wrapped in a friend's towel, my heart aching for the loss and also longing for the good that's coming. Not all stories begin broken and end whole. Most start somewhere in the middle, and they fumble forward, crashing and rising again. Most stories are wild travels along unknown trails, sometimes in the dark and sometimes toward the rising dawn.

I walk the sidewalk, blasted by the San Franciscan wind. I think of the street sign and whisper, "Lead us, Spirit. From here to there. From here to there."

The Great Silence

There comes a moment when attention must be paid.
. . . A time to embrace mystery as my native land. And
silence as my native tongue.

—John Kirvan

August, Twentieth Week of Ordinary Time

Austin, Texas

Tonight Chris gives August a bath in our temporary apartment, and I strap Brooksie, my five-month-old who has just begun sitting up and reaching for his brother's toys, into the baby wrap. I walk out into the wide-open apartment complex, pushing a stroller full of recycling to its appropriate depository.

The air here is heavy. For so long I dreamed of heat, of bare legs and uncovered toes, and here I am, walking at 7:30 p.m. in 105-degrees over an endless asphalt parking lot. In the distance, the sunset flames. There is no sunset like a Texas sunset.

This afternoon, I took the boys to Chris's new office to eat lunch and meet some of his coworkers. A friend of his asked me how it feels to be back in Texas. I said, "You know, Texas is my home, but I only know how to be a kid here. I became a grown-up everywhere else."

Then I listened to those words in my head. Saying them again. Turning them around for a different view. And I agreed with myself. I was twenty-two when I left. A third of my life ago, I lived on this land, in this culture. I don't know how to be an adult here. I'm going to have to learn.

Brooksie and I walk. He doesn't mind the heat like the rest of us do. He doesn't notice the sunset. He only sees me, tilting his head back in the baby wrap, smiling. He reaches his hand up to touch my cheek.

"Hello, T-Rexy," I say. "Listen, I'm not asking for required composting. I know we're in Texas now. But you'd think Austin would be hippie enough that I wouldn't have to walk half a mile to recycle around here."

Brooksie waits for me to look in his eyes again. And when I do, he smiles wide.

I inhale deep then stare back out at the sky, thinking about Mama Mac, my great-grandmother who worked her West Texas farm in this weather, raising seven kids through the Dust Bowl, without an air conditioner, without a washing machine. It's strange to be here, where people around me talk the way my family talks, where boys and girls in the supermarket answer "Yes, ma'am" to the lady behind the checkout counter, just as I learned to do as a child.

I think about stability and remember it's time for prayer, for Compline, a prayer of gratitude, a prayer for rest.

> Let evening come upon us . . .
> let gentle rest descend.[1]

That sort of rest brings in *The Great Silence* as the monks move from group prayer to quiet loneliness. They walk that silent path to bed. They brush their teeth and lie on their beds asking God to show them their day, in all its beauty, in all its brokenness. Perhaps that gentle pattern, that daily motion of prayer, morning to night, is what really shapes stability.

Perhaps what roots me to a land is not the happenings I knew in that space. Not the babies born or grown there. Not the memories made on sidewalks, the faces recognized at the playground. Not the temperature of the wind or the nearness of the ocean. Here in this state where my ancestors built the lives that built me, I feel formed to the land just as animals fit themselves to a climate. Perhaps stability is here in the hours, in the markings of time, in the coming back to the God who loves me, the God I choose right now, here, where I am only a speck of life underneath this bright pink sky.

Stability is in the wholehearted coming and coming and coming again. Prayer is not an act I perform, words I recite, a behavior I strive to maintain. It is a returning. It is a broken life finding healing, a misplaced soul recognizing home.

I arrive at the recycling bins and pull the bags out of the stroller. "Mama Mac would've understood what to do with this heat," I explain to Brooksie. She'd shake her head at it, I think. She'd say it was the hottest summer she'd ever seen. She'd pray for rain for the dried-out cotton crops. And then she'd send the kids out in the heat to get the chores done. She'd work in that blazing sun: scrubbing clothes, tending the vegetable garden, feeding the cows. Maybe on evenings like this, she and Papa stood on a porch and watched this kind of sunset, sighed relief over all those children scrubbed clean and under sheets in beds.

I let the bags of cans and plastic jugs clang into the bright blue bin. Then I walk into the red-orange sky and feel a settling in me, a root easing down.

⤙⤚

August meets me at the door. "Mama, will you come listen to Daddy's story with me?"

And the four of us sit on August's great big temporary bed; Chris holds *Little Pea*² on his lap. I prop Brooksie into a wobbly sitting position between his dad and me. August's head falls back against my chest. My leg drapes over their dad's. We listen to the story. In this unfamiliar apartment, in this always changing, stable place. The four of us listen.

Notes

Foreword
1. Psalm 136:1 NIV.

Preface
1. Kathleen Norris, *The Cloister Walk* (New York: Riverhead Books, 1996), xix.
2. Ibid.

Chapter 1
1. Jeremiah 6:16 NIV.

Chapter 2
1. Michael Harter, SJ, ed., *Hearts on Fire: Praying with Jesuits* (Chicago: Loyola Press, 2004), 21.
2. Jesus gets lost as a twelve-year-old and is found in the temple (Luke 2:48–51). The wedding runs out of wine and Mary asks Jesus to do something about it (John 2:1–10). She and her sons wait "outside" a place where Jesus is teaching in order to "seize him," concerned that he is "out of his mind." (This story is repeated, though without the direct "out of his mind" statement, in Matthew 12 and Luke 8.)
3. "The Rule of Saint Benedict," © Ampleforth Abbey Trustees 1997 in Robert Atwell et al., *The Benedictine Handbook* (Norwich, CT: Canterbury Press, an imprint of Hymns Ancient & Modern, 2003), 64.

Chapter 4
1. "The Rule of Saint Benedict," 97.
2. Ibid., 10.

Chapter 6
1. Saint Gregory the Great, *Life and Miracles of Saint Benedict* (Book Two of the Dialogues), trans. ODO J. Zimmermann OSB, and Benedict R. Avery OSB (Collegeville, MD: Liturgical Press, no date). During his time "dwelling in the cave," Benedict was overcome with lustful thoughts toward a woman from his past. In order to rid himself of thoughts of her, he threw his body into a patch of thorny bushes and rolled in them. Benedict would later tell his disciples he was never tempted toward lust again.

2. Mark 10, Matthew 19.

3. Benedict was born somewhere around AD 480 and left Rome for Subiaco sometime in AD 500. Carmen Acevedo Butcher, *Man of Blessing: A Life of Saint Benedict* (Brewster, MA: Paraclete Press, 2006), 13.

4. Butcher, *Man of Blessing,* 42–49, 59.

5. Brother Benet Tvedten OSB, *How to be Monastic and Not Leave Your Day Job: An Invitation to Oblate Life* (Brewster, MA: Paraclete Press, 2006), 6.

Chapter 8

1. Bobby Gross, *Living the Christian Year: Time to Inhabit the Story of God* (Downers Grove, IL: InterVarsity Press, 2009), 84.

2. Psalm 50:14.

Chapter 9

1. Psalm 19:1 NIV.

2. Isaiah 45:2–3 NIV.

3. Psalm 130:1.

4. "The Rule of Saint Benedict," 22.

Chapter 12

1. Dennis Okholm, *Monk Habits for Everyday People: Benedictine Spirituality for Protestants* (Grand Rapids: Brazos Press, 2007), 55, 89.

2. Jean-Pierre de Caussade, *The Sacrament of the Present Moment,* Kitty Muggeridge, trans. (San Francisco: Harper SanFrancisco, reissued 2009).

Chapter 13

1. Psalm 51:15.

2. Saint Gregory the Great, *Life and Miracles of Saint Benedict,* 19–20, 22–25.

3. Butcher, *Man of Blessing,* 21. Saint Gregory gives the date AD 594 in *Life and Miracles of Saint Benedict.*

4. Psalm 22:1 NIV.

5. Psalm 22:19 NIV.

6. "The Sinner's Prayer" is evangelical shorthand for the prayer of commitment to Christ. In the prayer, a person acknowledges Jesus as Lord, asks forgiveness for sin, and vows to follow Jesus from that point forward.

7. For example, Benedict said of children and adolescents in the monastery: "If they are guilty of bad behavior, then they should be subjected to severe fasting or sharp strokes of the rod" (Chapter 30). Also children "should be smacked" for "careless inattention" when reciting or responding to a Psalm in the oratory (Chapter 45).

8. Even while Benedict describes rather severe punishment for bad behavior, his concern for the young and the weak is atypical. In Chapter 37, Benedict states that the authority of the rule should reinforce

our natural instinct toward concern for the young and the old. "They should receive loving consideration." He also believes that often, "the Lord makes the best course clear to . . . the youngest" (Chapter 3) and that "the care of those who are sick . . . is an absolute priority, which must rank before every other requirement" (Chapter 36).

Chapter 14
1. John 20:24–25.
2. Ibid.

Chapter 15
1. Matthew 27:46.
2. "The Rule of Saint Benedict," 22.
3. Esther de Waal, *The Celtic Way of Prayer: The Recovery of the Religious Imagination* (New York: Image Books, 1997), 155.

Chapter 16
1. Charles Wesley, "Christ the Lord Is Risen Today," 1739.
2. Fernando Ortega & Rich Nibbe, "Sing to Jesus," © Word Music, LLC (a div. of Word Music Group, Inc.), Dejamesolo Music (Admin. by Word Music Group, Inc.) Rich Nibbe Songs.

Chapter 17
1. Peggy Rathman, *Good Night Gorilla* (New York: GP Putnam's Sons, 1994).
2. Andrew Peterson, "Hey Beautiful Girl," in Andrew Peterson and Randall Goodgame, *Slugs, Bugs and Lullabies*, 2006, 2011, Entertainment One, compact disc.

Chapter 18
1. "The Rule of Saint Benedict," 44.
2. Ibid.

Chapter 20
1. Traditional nursery rhyme.
2. "The Rule of Saint Benedict," 64, 75.

Chapter 22
1. Ephesians 3:18 NIV.
2. Joan Chittister, *Wisdom Distilled from the Daily: Living the Rule of St. Benedict Today* (San Francisco: HarperOne, 1990), 151.
3. Ibid., 7.

Chapter 24
1. "I Have Decided to Follow Jesus," lyrics attributed to S. Sunder Singh, music Hindustani melody, public domain.
2. "I Surrender All," lyrics by J. W. Van Deventer, 1896. Music by W. S. Weeden, 1896. Public domain.

3. "Just As I Am," lyrics by Charlotte Elliott, 1835. Music by William Bradbury, 1849. Public domain.

4. James 1:17 KJV.

5. "Great Is Thy Faithfulness," lyrics by Thomas O. Chisholm. Music by William M. Runyan. © 1923, renewed 1951 by Hope Publishing Co., Carol Stream, IL 60188. For permission to reproduce hopepublishing. com.

Chapter 25

1. Parker Palmer, *The Politics of the Brokenhearted: On Holding the Tensions of Democracy* (Kalamazoo, MI: Fetzer Institute, 2005), 3.

Chapter 27

1. Psalm 15:1.

Chapter 28

1. Psalm 10:4 NIV.
2. Psalm 19:1–4 NIV.
3. Psalm 19:14 NIV.
4. Psalm 19:9–10 NIV.

Chapter 29

1. Esther de Waal, *The Celtic Way of Prayer: The Recovery of the Religious Imagination* (New York: Image, Doubleday, 1997), 48.
2. Ibid.
3. David Whyte, *Crossing the Unknown Sea: Work as a Pilgrimage of Identity* (New York: Riverhead Trade, 2002), 132.

Chapter 30

1. De Waal, *The Celtic Way of Prayer*, 47–48.
2. James Taylor, "Sweet Baby James," *Sweet Baby James*, Warner Bros., 1970.

Chapter 33

1. 2 Timothy 4:7.
2. "The Rule of Saint Benedict," 80–82, citing Psalm 119:116 NAB.
3. Tom Wright, *Paul for Everyone: The Pastoral Letters, 1 and 2 Timothy and Titus* (London: Westminster John Knox Press, 2003, 2004).

Chapter 38

1. Matthew 7:7.

Chapter 39

1. Psalm 90:14.
2. A paraphrase of 1 Peter 1:15–16.

Chapter 40

1. Czeslaw Milosz, "After Paradise," from *The Collected Poems* (Hopewell, NJ: Ecco Press, 1988), 395.
2. Numbers 6:24–26 NIV.
3. Psalm 15:1.

Chapter 43

1. Butcher, *Man of Blessing,* 83, 141.
2. "Rule of Saint Benedict," 96.
3. See 1 Corinthians 11:24–25.
4. Michael Casey, *A Guide to Living in the Truth* (Liguori: Liguori/ Triumph, 1999, 2001), 130.

Chapter 45

1. Elizabeth O'Connor, *Servant Leaders, Servant Structures* (Dallas: Potter's House, 1991).
2. Macrina Wiederkehr, *Seven Sacred Pauses: Living Mindfully Through the Hours of the Day* (Notre Dame, IN: Ave Maria Press, Sorin Books, 2008), 114.

Afterword

1. Judith Browser, OSB, in Wiederkehr, *Seven Sacred Pauses,* 149.
2. Amy Krouse Rosenthal, *Little Pea* (San Francisco: Chronicle Books, 2005).

About the Author

Micha (pronounced "MY-cah") Boyett is a writer, blogger, and sometimes poet. She was a contributor to the book *Talking Taboo: American Christian Women Get Frank About Faith*. A born and raised Texan, Micha lives in San Francisco with her husband, Chris, and their two sons. Learn more at www.michaboyett.com.

WORTHY
PUBLISHING

If you enjoyed this book, will you consider sharing the message with others?

- Mention the book in a Facebook post, Twitter update, Pinterest pin, or blog post.

- Recommend this book to those in your small group, book club, workplace, and classes.

- Head over to facebook.com/worthypublishing, "LIKE" the page, and post a comment as to what you enjoyed the most.

- Tweet "I recommend reading #Found by @michaboyett // @worthypub"

- Pick up a copy for someone you know who would be challenged and encouraged by this message.

- Write a book review online.

You can subscribe to Worthy Publishing's newsletter at worthypublishing.com.

WORTHY PUBLISHING
FACEBOOK PAGE

WORTHY PUBLISHING
WEBSITE